THE SCHOOLING OF CHILDREN OF CARIBBEAN HERITAGE

Kamala Nehaul

tb

Trentham Books

First published in 1996 by Trentham Books Limited

Trentham Books Limited
Westview House
734 London Road
Oakhill
Stoke-on-Trent
Staffordshire
England ST4 5NP

British Cataloguing in Publication Data
A catalogue record for this book is available from the British Library
ISBN: 1 85856 045 4

Designed and typeset by Trentham Print Design Ltd., Chester and printed in Great Britain by BPC Wheatons Ltd, Exeter

Contents

Acknowledgements

Writing a book for the first time is not easy. I am indebted to my family and friends, for the research could not have been done without their support. My parents' enthusiasm for the project throughout and the interest in its progress by my sons and husband, sustained me through many difficulties. The early months of data processing and computer breakdowns were stressful and my older's son support and advice at this stage was invaluable.

Bea Jaspars, my friend and colleague in Oxford, read key sections and helped also in the thankless task of proof reading. My husband, Ben Nehaul-Harris, spent endless hours editing, and my colleague Gillian Klein devoted much time to making the manuscript accessible to the general reader.

My thanks are due to Professor Sally Tomlinson of Goldsmiths' College, University of London, to Jagdish Gundara of the Institute of Education, University of London, to Barry Troyna of the University of Warwick, to my brother Dr. Lika Nehaul, and to my friend and colleague Cas Walker of the Education Department in Birmingham. They read the manuscript and made many useful suggestions Any remaining omissions or deficiencies are entirely my responsibility.

I carried out the fieldwork while working as a Research Fellow at the ESRC-funded Centre for Research in Ethnic Relations, University of Warwick. I would like to thank the staff at all levels who helped me while I was there. Finally, the research would not have been possible without the children and the teachers at the schools where the research was done. A special thank you to them.

Preface

I have written this book for academics and for parents and teachers. The summary is included to help readers find their way through the variety of material in it.

The book sets out to clarify an issue that has long been debated: whether and how the experiences of children of Caribbean heritage at school differ from those of their classmates and the influences on their academic achievement.

An increasing number of schools in Britain have pupils of Caribbean background. Some are high achievers but many underachieve. Examining factors which foster or hinder achievement is particularly relevant at a time when all children are entitled to the national curriculum and academic attainment is measured and emphasised as a priority.

Chapter 1 sets the scene describing the number and regional distribution of black British pupils of Caribbean heritage and examining also their cultural backgrounds. Can there be differences in culture of which teachers are not sufficiently aware? The chapter summarises the research which justifies a continuing concern about underachievement.

Despite studies dating back to the early nineteen-sixties, we have no firm conclusions about the key reasons for underachievement. Chapter 2 describes the research theories suggested to explain underachievement and looks critically at trends in research.

Chapters 3 to 7 describe research carried out by the author in the spring and summer terms of 1992 in five primary classrooms. All were 'positive classrooms', i.e. located in schools where teachers were genuinely interested in ensuring that equal opportunities be available for their ethnic minority pupils. Chapter 3 describes the design of the research. Chapter 4 combines teacher perceptions of twenty-five pupils with the author's observations, to identify the pupil factors which influence achievement. The twenty-five pupils are all of Caribbean heritage and cover a range of abilities, personal attributes and home backgrounds.

Chapter 5 examines the teachers' perceptions of home and pupil variables and concludes that these do not support a deficit theory of underachievement. The next chapter is made up of the author's observations of classrooms, children's responses to multicultural projects, and the teachers' philosophies about classroom strategies, in an attempt to identify classroom factors which contribute positively to achievement. Observations are also analysed to see whether the treatment of pupils of Caribbean heritage in these positive classrooms is in any way unfair or different from that received by other pupils.

In chapter 7, pupils' experiences arising from their 'race' and background are examined in the light of qualitative data covering a range of activities in classrooms and other parts of the school. Although school is generally a positive experience for pupils of Caribbean heritage, a large proportion of the year 2 pupils in the author's research appear to have negative experiences associated with 'race' and background and implications of this for their achievement is examined. Lastly, conclusions from the individual case studies are used to evaluate the teachers' views about the pupils.

The main purpose of chapter 8 is to clarify what conclusions can be drawn from previously published research on racism. Racism in action, its complexity and the difficulties of researching this area are scrutinised, and processes through which teacher racism may contribute to underachievement are identified.

Chapter 9 draws together all the complexthreads of the argument to suggest a new theory and ways of promoting the achievement of children of Caribbean heritage.

Chapter 1

Introduction

The major phase of immigration to Britain from the Caribbean started in the late forties. In 1947, the Ormonde arrived with 100 people from Jamaica and, in 1948, the Empire Windrush brought in another 492. Immigration continued in the fifties, accelerated just before immigration controls were introduced in the early sixties and began to fall thereafter. By 1966 the number of people in Britain born in the Caribbean was about 300,000 (Rose, 1969), more than half of them from Jamaica. By 1973, immigration was in effect over (Peach, 1991).

Migration was partly a response to employment conditions in the countries of origin but a key influence on the movement to Britain was the need in Britain for labour. Its origins lay in war-time recruitment, and it was shaped by recruitment of people to work for British Rail, London Transport and the Health Service after the war (Peach, 1991). Initially, immigrants came mainly from Jamaica, then from Barbados and, as time progressed, from Trinidad and other countries in the Caribbean (Peach, 1991).

The 1961 census shows that there were 98,600 Caribbean immigrants settled in London. More than half of those from Jamaica settled there, as did large numbers from other parts of the Caribbean. A lesser but significant area of settlement was the West Midlands. Other conurbations also

	Jamaica	Rest of Caribbean
Greater London Conurbation	53,300	45,300
West Midlands Conurbation	20,100	4,700
All Conurbations	(80,300)	(55,300)
Elsewhere	19,800	16,500
Total (England & Wales)	100,100	71,800
Source: Rose, 1969, from the 1961 census		

attracted immigrants, especially West Yorkshire and Merseyside. Overall, about 80% settled in conurbations.

By the 1991 census, many of those of 'Caribbean background' were British and had been born in Britain. A total of 677,900 people in Britain identified themselves as black-Caribbean or as black-Other (Owen, 1992). A further 207,500 identified themselves as black-African though the immediate origin of some of these was the Caribbean rather than Africa. So in all, there were probably about 750,000 thousand people of Caribbean background living in Britain in 1991.

Their geographic distribution was fairly similar to that in 1961, with a large proportion living in urban areas (Owen, 1992). This is reflected in the regional distribution of those aged 5-15 in England (see opposite). The total figure of 123,400 does not allow for those designated as 'black-African' whose immediate origin was the Caribbean. So there may be about 130,000 children of Caribbean background in England in the age group 5-15 in the nineteen nineties. As shown in the table above, many live in London or in metropolitan authorities especially, in the case of the latter, in the urban areas around Birmingham, Leeds, Manchester and Liverpool.

Despite the concentration in more urbanised areas, the 1991 census figures suggest that children of Caribbean background also live in other parts of the country. The non-metropolitan authorities account for more than a fifth of the total. A breakdown of statistics by local education authorities, (not given here) shows that individual authorities in the

2

Census Population, Aged 5-15		
	Black-Caribbean and Black-Other	Black-African
London	66,100	28,100
Metropolitan of which:	29,400	3,500
West Midlands	(16,600)	(800)
South Yorks	(1,600)	(300)
West Yorks	(3,900)	(500)
Greater Manchester	(5,400)	(1,100)
Merseyside	(1,600)	(700)
Tyne and Wear	(300)	(100)
Non-Metropolitan	27,900	4,600
Total (England)	123,400	36,100
Source: Dr Owen, from the 1981 Census		

Northern Region, the North West, Yorkshire and Humberside, and the South West, have some children of Caribbean background, albeit small numbers — typically less than 500. A further breakdown by districts within each authority, whether metropolitan or county, again not shown, suggests that children within an authority may be thinly spread through many of its districts.

Four Decades of Experience

For those who arrived from the Caribbean, life was far from easy. Adults and children had to cope at times with hostility from the 'traditional' inhabitants of Britain. Many were likely to be disadvantaged in housing and employment. This has been well documented in statistical analyses and, more poignantly, in the personal accounts of those who came to Britain and in their literature, poetry and drama (Cottle, 1978; Carter, 1986; Berry, 1986; Dodgson, 1984).

Decades later, socio-economic disadvantage is still a reality for many. As has become increasingly clear, racism plays a part in this and contributes also to the disadvantage encountered in a range of other areas including for example immigration practices, mental health provision, police action and the criminal justice system.

In education, the situation is and has been very complex. As will be seen in later chapters, the role played by racism in schools has been debated at length. The processes through which racism can affect children's educational experiences have not been easy to decipher and there is by no means a consensus about the nature of racism or even about how it is defined. Nevertheless, there are differences in the educational experiences of pupils of Caribbean background and white pupils for, as the evidence described below shows, there are less favourable academic outcomes for pupils of Caribbean background.

Fairly soon after children began to arrive in Britain, it became apparent that something was wrong. Initially attention concentrated on their excessive allocation to classes and schools for the educationally sub-normal (ESN schools). As time progressed, it emerged that children of Caribbean background, as a group, were doing less well in external examinations than white children, and examination results became a major concern.

The first official recognition of the need to monitor achievement occurred in 1981 when the Rampton Report was published (Department of Education and Science, 1981). Using 1978 statistics on school leavers in five authorities, the Report highlighted the poor performance of pupils of Caribbean background. One illustration of their less good performance was that proportionately fewer received five or more high grades in O-Level and CSE examinations than did children overall in the same authorities.

The statistics in the Rampton Report and the analysis of these merely added to the dauntingly large body of evidence collected since the late sixties. The studies that gave the evidence of underachievement varied considerably in their scope and in the data used. Some used psychometric tests. Some analysed group tests of performance in reading and in verbal and non-verbal reasoning. Occasionally, the focus was on achievement in mathematics. The under-representation of pupils of Caribbean background in grammar schools and in higher streams and sets was examined. Their over-representation in ESN schools and classes was highlighted. Examination results were analysed by ethnic origin. (See reviews in Taylor, 1981 and Tomlinson, 1983.)

The design of studies varied. Some were small-scale, others large-scale. Some used national data, others regional. Many used cross-section data but there were a few longitudinal studies (Taylor, 1981; Tomlinson, 1983).

While some of the research was open to criticism, not least for size and design, the general consensus in 1981 was that the research indicated that pupils of Caribbean background were underachieving (Taylor, 1981). The Rampton Report gave additional credence to the reality of underachievement (Department for Education and Science, 1981). Further confirmation came with the publication of a critical review by Tomlinson of work done in the period before the publication of the Rampton Report (Tomlinson, 1983).

Since 1981, there has been further research. Analyses of the distribution of pupils in ability sets arising from the banding, streaming and setting of pupils became less common after the introduction of comprehensive schools and the move away from ability grouping. But some such studies did take place, and the results were consistent with earlier work, confirming that pupils of Caribbean background were being disproportionately placed in lower sets compared with white pupils in the same schools (Scarr et al, 1983; Figueroa, 1991).

Research on examination results has continued : for example, by Kysel using ILEA schools in 1985 with nearly 3000 pupils of Caribbean background, by Drew and Gray using a national random sample in 1985 with results for 244 pupils of Caribbean background, by Smith and Tomlinson for 1985 examination results from 18 schools in four authorities with 146 pupils of Caribbean background, and by Nuttall and Goldstein using examination results for ILEA schools since 1985. A collation of results from these and earlier key studies indicates that statistics and the conclusions from their analysis are similar to Rampton's (Drew and Gray, 1991).

Also available are analyses by education authorities. The Inner London Education Authority (abolished on 31st March 1990) began to monitor its examination results in 1985. The ILEA was concerned about the achievement of pupils of Bangladeshi and Turkish origin as well as those of Caribbean backgrounds. These three groups performed below the average for the authority (ILEA Research and Statistics Branch, 1990). Some other authorities with an interest and commitment to equal opportunities began to do occasional or regular monitoring in the late eighties.

While it was agreed that children of Caribbean background were not attaining well academically, it was sometimes argued that this was not necessarily associated with their ethnicity or Caribbean backgrounds. The most long-standing issue has been whether levels of underachievement are connected, not to ethnicity, but to the fact that a large proportion of children of Caribbean background are 'working class'.

In practice, analyses which attempted to untangle class and ethnicity showed evidence of underachievement even when corrections have been made to allow for the effects of social class. One reviewer collated work published before the mid-eighties. This included work published in the seventies by Bagley, Payne, Little, and Essen and Ghodsian, and in the eighties by Mabey, Scarr, Craft and Craft, and Barnes (Hyder 1985). All of these indicated underachievement even after taking account of social class. Quantitative research published since the mid-eighties confirmed these earlier findings (Mortimore et al, 1988; Smith and Tomlinson, 1989; Drew and Gray, 1991).

Since the issue of class versus ethnicity is one which has been mis-understood and in some cases misrepresented, it is worth drawing atten-tion to this body of evidence supporting the view that underachievement is not purely a social class phenomenon. Interestingly, while an effort has been made to isolate the effect of race from that of class statistically, very little attention has been devoted to key questions. Are the attributes of the 'working class', as derived from reflection and research on the white population, mirrored by those said to be 'working class of Caribbean background'? Does there need to be research on the 'Caribbean working class' before one can hypothesise about the effect of class on education? Most important of all, is it *statistically* possible to separate ethnicity and class effects? The latter will be discussed in the concluding chapter of this book.

An issue which has become prominent more recently is that of gender. There is some evidence that girls of Caribbean background do relatively well compared with boys (See reviews by Tomlinson, 1983 and Mirza, 1992). But as in the case of class, though possibly for different reasons, the effect of gender has been misrepresented.

Tomlinson's review included work published before 1981. Ten years later, there is very little additional evidence. Mirza opened a chapter reviewing the research literature by saying that black girls do relatively well at school (Mirza, 1992). Yet she quoted only two studies which analyse statistics, one by Driver using data from students who left school in the late seventies, and an analysis of 1985 examination results from the Inner London Education Authority. Mirza claimed that her own research in two schools confirmed that girls do relatively well. For example, 5% of black girls obtained five or more higher grades while no boys, black or white, did so.

Mirza's conclusion that black girls do better may not be justified. One school in her sample was co-educational and said to be mediocre academically. All the boys involved must have attended this school as the second was a girls school. The sample of girls may have included some from the latter, a selective school, with a greater work ethos and, presumably, better examination results.

As far as I know, there are no other published research studies or recent education authority analyses by gender which show consistently higher achievement by girls of Caribbean heritage. So I dispute the claim that girls of Caribbean heritage do not underachieve.

In addition to debates on class and gender, there have been discussions about whether underachievement is due to the concentration of children of Caribbean background in inner city schools which may be less good academically. The theory that underachievement is primarily due to ineffective schools located in disadvantaged areas rather than to issues of ethnicity, is difficult to test adequately. There are as yet no data on poor inner city schools and the numbers of children of Caribbean background in them as compared with other schools. Yet the inner city theory of underachievement has been growing in popularity. So it is worth stressing that the 1991 census data, mentioned in the first section of this chapter, suggest that children of Caribbean background live in many different parts of the country and are by no means restricted to inner city areas.

Clearly then, in spite of the questions about class, gender and inner city effects, concern about underachievement is justified and should continue to be raised. Not surprisingly, interest in achievement is growing at a practical or policy level. Frequently this is in the context of monitoring achievement for ethnic minority groups encompassing those of Asian and Caribbean origin or other potentially disadvantaged groups. One example of this is to be found in the Report for Her Majesty's Inspectorate for 1990/1991. Based on the inspection of over 7000 institutions, it reported

7

worryingly low standards found in a number of specific groups. In its section on secondary schools, the Report drew attention to substantial underachievement in Key Stage 3 and GCSE and cited specifically the lack of success of boys of Caribbean background and of pupils of Bangladeshi origin (Department of Education and Science, 1992).

Since the National Curriculum was introduced, data have been available at a national level for younger pupils. As the assessment of seven year olds at Key Stage 1 commenced, results have been analysed by ethnic origin. The 'Consortium for Assessment and Testing in Schools' Report for 1990 concluded that children of ethnic minority origin were doing less well, and the 'Evaluation for National Curriculum Testing' Report from the Leeds University School of Education concluded, more specifically, that performance in English and maths by ethnic minority groups was less good than for others (Consortium for Assessment and Testing in Schools, 1991; University of Leeds School of Education, 1991).

More recently, the National Federation for Educational Research/ Bishop Grosseteste College Consortium reported for 1992 that in their research, which included a small sample of children from ethnic minority groups, black and Asian pupils were more likely to attain level 1 or below and less likely to attain level 2 or level 3 in English or maths (NFER/BGC Consortium, 1992).

There are also analyses at education authority level, involving occasional and in some cases regular monitoring of examination results and/or National Curriculum Key Stage 1 results for the authority. Reports seen by the author suggest that there is a slightly greater tendency to focus on pupils of Asian rather than Caribbean background. This may be because the implementation of the national curriculum has highlighted difficulties in assessing bilingual learners. Nevertheless, some work has been done on pupils of Caribbean background and, as is true for the studies mentioned earlier, these justify a concern about their underachievement.

As part of my work as an achievement project manager, I have assisted in the analysing of GCSE results for project schools. My data suggests that underachievement is changing. In some schools, there are proportionately fewer students of Caribbean heritage than five years ago, who are not entered for exams or fail to complete them. However, relatively few students of Caribbean heritage receive the highest GCSE grades, and the distribution by grade suggests that many students of Caribbean heritage obtain a grade which is two levels below what might be expected. Thus continuing concern may be warranted even even in areas with a commitment to improvement.

Awareness of underachievement as an issue may have increased rather than decreased since schools have been being inspected in accordance with the Education (Schools) Act 1992. The official guidance materials on inspection contained a section on Equal Opportunities and evidence required included standards of achievement of individuals and groups (Department for Education, 1993 b). Accordingly, more schools and local authorities may have begun to monitor the achievement of pupils of ethnic minority backgrounds, including those of Caribbean origin (See pages 170-171, for developments since 1992).

Thus concern about underachievement by children of Caribbean background persists. Also disquieting today is the disproportionate number of these pupils who are excluded from schools because of poor behaviour. This was first highlighted in a report on the referral and suspension of pupils of Caribbean background from schools in Birmingham, published by the Commission for Racial Equality (1985).

Since then publicity has been given to other authorities where there appear to be problems e.g. Nottingham and London, and to research which highlights the disproportionate suspensions and other forms of sanctions meted out to pupils of Caribbean background, suggesting that these actions may often not be justified (Gillborn, 1990). More recently, a government publication on education for disaffected pupils reported that the 'number of pupils, especially boys, of Afro-Caribbean origin excluded is disproportionately higher than their white peers' (Department for Education, 1993 a).

The implications of such disciplinary action are worrying. The achievement of the children excluded unduly from the classroom will suffer, and a greater proportion are likely to fall into the category who are not entered for, or fail to complete, GCSE examinations. Also, excessive disciplinary action raises questions about why this happens and about whether this is the 'tip of an iceberg', with other pupils of Caribbean background in the schools concerned experiencing poor and unsympathetic pastoral care.

Summing up, although families of Caribbean background have been in Britain for four decades, concern about the academic achievement of their children has continued and is justified by research. This, plus pastoral concerns highlighted relatively recently, suggests that children of Caribbean background suffer from educational disadvantage in schools.

Issues in the Measurement of Underachievement

It is often said that the extent of underachievement has been diminishing over the decades since the earliest years of immigration. That this may be the case was argued in the Swann Report on the basis of comparisons of the data in the Interim (Rampton) and the Final (Swann) Report. While it is difficult to find other published data on trends, some reduction of underachievement with time seems plausible. This does not, however, mean that the underachievement of children of Caribbean heritage, as a group and in all areas of Britain, has been eliminated. As argued in the last section, continuing concern is justified.

Whether the degree of underachievement varies with the age of pupils has also been considered in measuring underachievement. In the earlier phases of concern, and especially with evidence from examination results, there was an interest in whether younger British-born pupils underachieved and also in the age at which underachievement starts. The variation of underachievement in relation to age has been difficult to examine since it requires longitudinal data for individual pupils but recently published research based on longitudinal data suggests that problems occur in the primary stage of schooling (Sammons, 1995). Other evidence comes from a recent analysis of National Curriculum results in a Metropolitan Authority which suggests that children of Caribbean background start school ahead of others in the basics, implying that underachievement at a later stage must reflect disadvantages faced at school from the very earliest years of schooling (*Sunday Times*, 1994)

It has also been suggested that it is important to examine underachievement in specific curricular areas. The Smith and Tomlinson research indicated that children of Caribbean background performed less well in maths than white children in the sample schools although performance in English did not indicate underachievement (Smith and Tomlinson, 1989). Other researchers have also suggested that maths may be a problem in some cases while performance in English compares reasonably well with that of white pupils in the same schools (Sammons, 1995).

More important is the need to look further at the most appropriate statistical measure to use for underachievement. Some researchers who have analysed and compared exam results for different groups in recent years use bar charts to represent and compare the percentage distribution by grade for specific subjects. Others look especially at the percentage of pupils of Caribbean background obtaining higher grades in specific subjects, or the percentage obtaining five or more high grades. Occasionally, the median is derived. A single aggregate measure is sometimes calculated, by weighting and aggregating the grade obtained in each subject.

In a few cases, the indication of lesser achievement by pupils of Caribbean background may depend on the method used for analysis. It has been argued that with the use of a bar chart or the percentage of higher grades, the degree of academic underachievement can be exaggerated, leading to incorrect findings of underachievement. It is therefore argued that a single aggregate measure may be preferable to examining bar charts or distributions (Drew and Gray, 1990).

However, I would challenge this argument because one cannot ignore inequalities at one end of the distribution if they exist. The exclusive use of a weighted average which may hide such inequalities depending on the weights employed, or the use of a median which effectively puts a lower value on scores at the extremes of the distribution, is questionable.

These are all important issues. But since the evidence on underachievement seems to justify concern, the most immediate and pressing need is to focus on the real and current issue of what to do to promote achievement and raise standards. This book focuses therefore on the latter rather than looking more deeply at measurement issues.

Finally, the use of the term 'underachievement' has been criticised on the grounds that it has connotations suggesting that the problems lie with the 'underachievers'. The term 'inequality' or 'educational disadvantage' is deemed more accurate (Figueroa, 1991; Wright, 1987; Troyna,1990). 'Underachievement' may also give the impression that there are no achievers amongst pupils of Caribbean background. Since these seem valid comments, this book refers wherever possible to 'achievement' qualified as relevant or, where appropriate, to 'educational disadvantage'.

Cultural Roots

Before discussing the aims and focus of this book, it is important to reflect on children of Caribbean background and, in particular, on cultural backgrounds and whether children in this group are 'different' from white pupils.

The term Caribbean commonly refers to what were originally British colonies. There are the ten 'island' countries — Antigua, Barbados, Dominica, Grenada, Jamaica, Montserrat, St Kitts/Nevis/Anguilla, St Lucia, St Vincent, Trinidad and Tobago. Then there is Guyana, on the mainland of South America. Sometimes the term has a wider meaning and may include the French islands of Guadeloupe and Martinique and other islands. Geographically, it should include all countries around the Caribbean Sea but, in Britain, it is usually applied to only the ten islands and Guyana.

The countries of the Caribbean differ significantly because of differing histories and differences in their contact with the four colonisers. Britain, France, Spain, and Holland competed for territory and wealth in the seventeenth and eighteenth centuries and, with the exception of Barbados, the colonies were at some time owned by one or more colonisers other than Britain. (See Mitchener, 1989 for a historical novel on this subject.) This led to differences in for example the Caribbean creoles. Thus, the influence of France and French is most noticeable today in the creoles used in St Lucia and Dominica (Dalphinis, 1986), which are very different to those spoken in countries influenced predominantly by Britian (Cassidy, 1971). Creoles in the latter have more in common, although they are noticeable differences even amongst these in the vocabulary, grammar and intonation.

In many countries the majority population have African roots. There are also people of Indian descent of whom the greatest numbers live in Guyana and Trinidad, where they account for nearly half the population. The 'white' population was and is relatively small and consists of descendants of planters from the colonising countries, those offered asylum in the course of battles for territory, indentured servants from Portugal and Britain, and a sprinkling of pirates from Britain. There are people whose forefathers originated from China and Syria, some of them relatively recently. And there are the descendants of the original inhabitants, and large numbers of people who are a mix of many different backgrounds.

Food, customs, music and folklore are broadly similar across the Caribbean but with variations depending on the mix of origins and developments within countries. The rich and varied heritage led to a distinct Caribbean cuisines, for instance, with recipes that vary between countries, partly because of different cultural histories. Stories, music and customs were also affected. For example, the Anansi or Brother Nancy stories, from the Ashanti in Africa, are found throughout, but Trinidad and Guyana also have a heritage of stories from India.

Carnival, the street festival celebrating the end of Lent, used to be associated exclusively with Trinidad, while John Canoe was observed at Christmas time in Jamaica and Guyana. Both originated from the mix of African culture and the colonial experience. Steel bands and calypso evolved in Trinidad and, until recently, reggae was the music of Jamaica. In Trinidad and Guyana music derived from the Asian sub-continent is played and enjoyed.

Differences within the Caribbean were maintained because of limited contact between the countries, which persisted until the late fifties. Links were with the European nations with whom their main trade occurred, rather than with other parts of the Caribbean.

If we look at religion, we find differences again, with Catholicism more significant in Trinidad and St Lucia, where the influence of Spain and/or France was great. Interestingly, but perhaps not surprisingly in view of the original mix of peoples, there is also great diversity within countries. In Jamaica, for example, one writer mentions Anglicans, Baptists, Quakers, Presbyterians and Roman Catholics, accounting for about three-quarter of the religious denominations in the 1940s and, amongst the remainder, Moravians, Adventists, Church of God Members, Pentecostal, Evangelical, Hindu, and Pocomania (Hendriques, 1953). In Trinidad, Roman Catholics, Hindus and Anglicans account for about three-quarters of the population, and the rest includes Muslims, Presbyterians, Adventists, Methodists, Baptists and Church of God members (Dabydeen and Samaroo, 1987).

In all, then, the Caribbean of the fifties and sixties, i.e. at the time of immigration, showed considerable diversity between and within countries. There were many commonalities however, and one could argue that there was also a common Caribbean culture.

When the 'traditional culture' in Britain is compared with a minority culture, the tendency is to look for major differences between them in language, dress, religion and food, and to ignore diversity within the minority culture. This has occurred when reflecting on the Caribbean. And with an emphasis on the apparent similarity of Caribbean roots to white British culture, attention is deflected from differences, including fundamental ones in some aspects of culture.

Caribbean Cultural Backgrounds

'Culture' is wide-ranging, incorporating the shared knowledge and ideas of a group of people. These underlie behaviour, not only social behaviour but also interpersonal behaviour. In effect, culture provides a sort of coding, setting boundaries for what is acceptable, proper and understandable at an individual level, within the family and the wider community. Thus, as well as the language spoken and the religion practiced, an examination of 'culture' needs to embrace attitudes and beliefs, ideas about right and wrong, about proper and improper behaviour and common understandings. The method and interpretation of interpersonal communication are influenced by culture, as are interfamily and intercommunity relationships and expectations about roles and responsibilities.

Seen in this light, the culture of those arriving from the Caribbean might have differed significantly from that which they encountered in the urban areas of Britain in which they settled. Differences in communication might have arisen not just from creole but from the style and content of conversation, non-verbal cues and from the etiquette underlying what was said and how.

Research on Caribbean culture and society in the sixties and seventies focused on social groupings, in particular those connected with class and colour, and on family structure (Clarke, 1966; Hendriques, 1953; Horowitz, 1971; Lowenthall, 1971). In researching family structures, relevant economic and historic influences were considered but analyses did not and have still not looked at the overall cultural framework and the underlying values.

Discussions with people from the Caribbean about families and communities suggests that there may have been differences in certain basic

14

value systems. In particular there was probably an assumption of greater interdependence and at the same time more formal and hierarchical systems within Caribbean families and communities. Interdependence and a structured hierarchy were beneficial and underpinned aspects of child rearing. Children contributed to family tasks and were expected to be disciplined and responsible. Importance was attached to having a role but also to enjoyment, talking and sharing as part of the family, often an extended one. 'Playing' had its place within this system.

Another distinct cultural characteristic mentioned by people from the Caribbean was the value placed on education. It was seen as an important vehicle for self-improvement, and girls and boys were encouraged to work hard at school and strive for the best possible qualifications to enhance their life chances.

Thus people arriving from the Caribbean brought with them their own culture, a very diverse culture that was, at the same time, distinct from white British culture. Aspects of food, music and religion differed, though there were many overlaps with the customs of the white British population. And there were significant and sometimes subtle differences in relationships, expectations, communication and values.

Children/Pupils of Caribbean Heritage

Children or adults whose families originate from the Caribbean are often referred to as being 'of Caribbean background', and this practice has been followed so far in this book. The author prefers the term 'of Caribbean heritage' and will use it frequently henceforth. The phrase 'children of Caribbean heritage' is assumed to include those with one or more parents or grandparents from the Caribbean.

Many people 'of Caribbean heritage' in Britain are primarily of African ancestry (referred to in Britain as 'Afro-Caribbean' or African-Caribbean) but because of the mixed ethnic composition of the population in the Caribbean, they could also be of Indian, Chinese and sometimes white British ancestry, or a mix of ethnicities.

Reflections on Cultures and Differences

With the continuing concern over the years about achievement by children of Caribbean heritage and the ensuing analyses of causes and solutions, discussions sometimes centred on culture. There were many ambiguities and contradictions. In some cases, specific aspects of families of Caribbean heritage were discussed, even though the tendency was to emphasise the similarity between Caribbean and white British culture.

When focusing on similarities, the lesser achievement of pupils of Caribbean heritage seemed particularly surprising. Why should 'under-achievement' continue once families and children of Caribbean heritage had overcome the shock of emigration? In the case of children originating from the Asian sub-continent, culture was appreciably different and language could be seen as a major barrier to achievement. But many thought that this was not the case with children of Caribbean heritage.

The suggestion that British children of Caribbean heritage might be no different from white British children appears even more plausible in the nineteen nineties. Some children may be of Caribbean-born grandparent-age, some may have a mix of Caribbean-born and white grandparents; for others their parents or, in some cases, one parent will have come from the Caribbean, mostly in the sixties or early seventies as young adults or children, to join parents or other family members. Thus pupils today have been born and brought up in Britain, and are often more than one generation removed from their Caribbean roots. They may never have visited the Caribbean, and many might have a parent or grandparents who are white. It could be argued that families of Caribbean heritage will be increasingly adapting to their local British cultures.

However, this is far too simplistic a picture. There are several reasons why those of Caribbean background might have retained some of their cultural heritage even if surrounded by white families with different values, norms and customs. Initially, families settled in areas where there were others from the Caribbean and wherever they lived, many had regular contacts with family and friends of Caribbean heritage in other parts of the country. In some cases families belonged to religious communities which had and have significant numbers of people of Caribbean heritage i.e. Black Churches consisting exclusively of followers from the Caribbean, also Seventh Day Adventist churches and some Catholic churches. Moreover, it became increasingly possible to buy Caribbean foods and other products which symbolised and emphasised roots. This must have contributed to a feeling of being Caribbean and hence to perpetuating Caribbean culture. Finally, the continual reminder to those of Caribbean heritage that they were 'different' might well have played its part.

Prejudice based on colour was not a new experience for those born in the Caribbean. But in the Caribbean they had been surrounded by other black people; there was a greater feeling of dignity and of being valued, and black people with a low or insecure income had a greater chance of upward mobility. Thus the effect of prejudice in Britain was felt much more acutely, with consequent feelings of rejection and anger — and this at a time of the 'black is beautiful' movement, which exhorted people of African descent to value themselves. Books, resources and artefacts encouraging the movement began to be available in shops.

Some families maintained close links with the Caribbean, visiting their families and friends and encouraging friends and family from the Caribbean to come to Britain on holiday. Thus have stories about the Caribbean gradually become part of the culture of many black British families and their children.

In short, continuing contact with like-minded others from a similar culture, the ability to buy culturally significant foods, materials and resources, ongoing contact with the Caribbean, and a growing anger fuelling feelings about the importance of one's background helped to ensure that some families retained the values and norms and common understandings of the Caribbean culture brought to Britain.

While retaining some of the cultural heritage brought from the Caribbean and a distinctness from the surrounding culture of a majority and rejecting group, the response to unfair treatment might have caused the culture of some to develop and change with a momentum founded in the history of slavery. This has left its legacy and its implications cannot be ignored. As one writer said:

> The confiscation of freedom made a terrific impact on Afro-Caribbean people. The forced-labour experience they endured — that not belonging to yourself, that endless no-pay work, that being ineligible for common rights that uphold human dignity, that way of life called slavery —translated itself into a burdensome loss. Freedom became a haunting thought and prayer and dream of Afro-Caribbean people. It aroused resistance. It has come to arouse a dynamic desire for reclamation (Berry, 1986).

Not surprisingly, people faced with racism in Britain increasingly tried to discover the past contributions of African and Caribbean people to history. Role models hitherto unknown were claimed as part of the cultural heritage and, for some families, became an important part of culture. Many are now included in publications. (See for example Bygott, 1993, who draws on a large selection.)

At another level, poetry and black British and Caribbean literature has flourished. This has built on the rich oral traditions of Caribbean culture and taken on 'all kinds of cultural, historical and social facts and data' about the Caribbean diaspora and its people (Berry, 1986). Again, aspects of this development are becoming an important element of the culture of some families of Caribbean heritage.

Another development was the growth of Rastafarianism. Often associated with the music of reggae and the youth resistance sub-culture, it developed rapidly in Britain in the seventies and dreadlocks became popular. Twenty years after the movement started, people of a range of ages and practices claim to be Rastas, white people among them.

Rastafarianism started in Jamaica. Essentially, it is a movement amongst people of African descent who look to Africa for roots, and perceive Jamaica and Britain as Babylon. The culture embodies a different and poetic use of language, and a development of traditional Caribbean culture and beliefs about roles, responsibilities and ways of life. In its purist form it is a religion and a way of life affirmed and perpetuated through regular meetings by families of Caribbean heritage.

At yet another level is the current 'ragamuffin' culture of some black youth of Caribbean origin. This has its roots in music and culture associated with the Caribbean heritage and is in effect a sub-culture. It may be more important to some young people than the culture of their families, whatever that might be. Like rastafarianism, the ragamuffin culture has became popularised because of its links with music, in this case rap, and is not restricted to people of Caribbean heritage.

In effect, the culture of people of Caribbean heritage in Britain in the nineteen nineties is not homogeneous. To the original Caribbean culture, with its subtle differences from white British culture and its diversity within, has been added other cultural threads and groupings. Perhaps even more than when the first settlers of Caribbean heritage came, it is essential to talk about cultures rather than culture. This is also true of 'white British culture' but white teachers are more likely to be aware of this.

Thus, just as in the early years of immigration, some aspects of the culture of children of Caribbean heritage may be distinct and different from the prevailing local culture of white British children. However, families are not homogeneous and different members may emphasise different aspects of their cultures. To complicate the picture further, some families may have adapted completely, their culture mirroring that of white British families, while in other families only some aspects of British culture will have become embedded in their ways of thinking. Amongst some white pupils, there will also have been changes as developing black culture(s) become absorbed into 'white' pupil culture.

In short, while the culture of some children of Caribbean heritage may be similar to that of white British children, for many others it may be different. An intercultural approach to education and teaching which aims to reflect children's culture in the classroom must take these complexities into account.

The Purpose of the Book

The school's arrangements for equality of opportunity are evaluated by the extent to which: all pupils irrespective of gender, ability (including giftedness), ethnicity, and social circumstances, have access to the curriculum and make the greatest progress possible (Department for Education, 1993b).

All children are entitled to the national curriculum and academic achievement is measured and emphasised as a priority, and this has implications for the 130,000 children of Caribbean background at school in England. Some perform very well academically, but there is evidence of continuing inequality for many and concerns also about undue exclusions.

For children of Caribbean heritage, the inequality which exists is associated partly with 'ethnicity' and cannot be explained away by gender, class and inner city effects. Pupils of Caribbean heritage are dispersed throughout a large proportion of education authorities in England and it is crucial that the schools and local authority staff involved be aware of the need for ethnic monitoring.

This book aims to clarify the causes of unequal outcomes for children of Caribbean heritage. Their school experiences may differ from those of white children. New research by the author and a review of previous ethnographic research on racism, suggest new approaches to achievement and strategies for equalising educational outcomes. Qualitative research in the eighties has largely been located in schools where teachers seem uncertain about pupils of Caribbean heritage, and in some cases, even hostile towards them. The author's research was located in 'positive' schools i.e. schools where the head and some teachers are committed to meeting the needs of ethnic minority pupils. Chapters 3 to 7 of the book are devoted to accounts of this research.

It is impossible to include an in-depth examination of all possible factors in one research study. Factors connected with homes are considered, analysed and built into the achievement model proposed at the end of the book. However, field work for chapters 3 to 7 was designed to focus on schools rather than homes as the main task was identifying what schools can do. The next step needs to be research focusing on families so as to test, confirm and extend the picture obtained here about the role of the home.

There are other areas which need to be examined in more depth than has been possible here, for example, 'culture' and the way that it can influence specific children's achievement. Secondly, the effects of class and gender have not been researched, though a start is made in the concluding chapter, which looks at the way their effects interweave with the effects of a Caribbean heritage. Both class and gender may have consequences which differ for those of Caribbean heritage and white pupils, and research on pupils of Caribbean heritage incorporating gender and class differences would be helpful. Also needed is more research on how academic achievement is measured and compared.

There are other important issues not discussed here. No attempt is made to compare the performance of pupils of Caribbean heritage with that of groups from the Asian sub-continent, or to discuss similarities and differences in their experiences and the effect of this on their achievement. Another area for separate research is the potential role and effect of black teachers. The educational experiences of students of Caribbean heritage in Further and Higher Education have also not been considered.

The book starts with a chapter giving a critical review of theories used to explain 'underachievement'. Chapters 3 to 7 are key chapters describing the author's research. After a chapter looking at existing and published research on racism, the book concludes with a chapter setting out an alternative model and strategies for schools wishing to promote the achievement of pupils of Caribbean background, and methodological issues for researchers to consider. For, as this book so clearly demonstrates, there is still much to be done to ensure that children of Caribbean heritage receive their full entitlement to education.

Chapter 2

Theories of Achievement

Black British children of Caribbean heritage, as a group, perform less well academically than some other groups of pupils. This was evident in the nineteen fifties and has continued in spite of some improvements. This chapter gives a critical review of the theories offered in explanation, and the development of ideas by academics and researchers. Such studies date back to the early sixties. Yet, in spite of decades of analysis, research has failed to give suitable guidance on causes of 'underachievement' and strategies to eliminate them and lack of achievement continues to cause concern.

The Rampton Report (1981) initiated a major change in the conceptualisation of the education of black pupils by highlighting the need to include the effect of racism in explaining ethnic minority achievement, so legitimitising the use of the term 'racism'. This chapter describes theories about pupils of Caribbean heritage that predate Rampton, and those investigated by researchers in the years which followed. Other research areas and changes in the underlying educational philosophy have implications for the progress of research on achievement and these are also examined.

23

Early Encounters

With the arrival of pupils from the Caribbean in schools in England came difficulties inherent in the different perceptions and expectations of those involved. Parents arriving from the Caribbean expected a good education for their children in the 'Motherland' as part of the package of moving to Britain (see, interalia, Carter 1986). Schools and the education system in Britain were uncertain about the new population, and concerned about the effect on the education of the indigenous pupils. Not surprisingly, there were clashes.

Black parents were faced in the 1960s with bussing and dispersal policies by local education authorities, and became increasingly aware of the disproportionate placement of their children in schools for the educationally sub-normal (ESN Schools. See Coard, 1971). As time progressed, they also became concerned at the failure of children in the mainstream schools. Pressure groups were formed to negotiate with the authorities to improve educational provision. The black educational movement accelerated as more of those in the black community realised that their children were not achieving as they should in British schools. Supplementary schools were set up to teach and support children out of school hours (Chevannes and Reeves, 1987).

In contrast, the mainstream schools attended by the new pupils were faced with sudden changes, for example children who were perceived as not fitting in easily, and families that teachers did not understand or relate to. They defined their concerns in terms of 'immigrant' problems (Green, 1985). Language deficit, cultural and family differences, the shock of immigration and poor home-school contacts were some of the problems identified by studies initiated by the Inner London Education Authority, where immigrants settled in the mid sixties. These studies fostered fears that educational standards were deteriorating due to increasing numbers of immigrants and spoke of:

> teacher energy being diverted to immigrants and able white families leaving ILEA (Tomlinson, 1983).

The researchers primarily identified the new immigrants as the problem, in some cases looking back at the countries of origin. One of the first reviews of literature on education and the new arrivals refers to a study in 1961 by Vernon, on the intellectual development of boys in the

Caribbean, which concluded that children's development was being handicapped by:

poor socio-economic, cultural and linguistic environment, defective education, and family instability (Goldman and Taylor, 1966).

Although aware that the immigrants faced prejudice, Goldman and Taylor saw the basic problem as associated with homes. They linked the 'plight of coloured immigrant children' in Britain with that of:

socially disadvantaged children in slum and problem areas, but with the added dimensions of language difficulties and colour prejudice to overcome.

From their survey of literature in 1966, they concluded that children of Caribbean origin most vividly illustrated problems of the immigrant groups, for while:

linguistically, they seem to have an advantage... it is their partial mastery of English, and their use of dialect which seems to be a major barrier to educational motivation and achievement. They also appear to be more susceptible to the climate, in terms of health, and pose difficulties for the host community because of the high incidence of broken families or children of varied parentage... authoritarian, or other climates within the family, affect attitudes to education. (Goldman and Taylor, 1966)

The extent to which families and homes were perceived as the problem is illustrated by the areas researched in an article published in the mid seventies. Under scrutiny were employment conditions, housing, marital status and the extent to which the family had been split up by emigration. Disorder and deviance in parents were considered. The research focused also on marital relations, the parent-child relationship, parental warmth, communication between parent and child, and the extent to which children confided in parents. Other areas examined were child-minding facilities, discipline at home, allocation of tasks to children at home, the education of parents, family contact with kin, and services contacted (Rutter et al, 1975). The list speaks for itself, reflecting the degree of uncertainty about the new population and the many areas in which they were seen as potentially deficient.

25

The research was thorough, detailed, and detached. The socio-economic disadvantage experienced by families of Caribbean heritage was confirmed, but the unexpected conclusion was the extent of similarity found in the cultures of West Indian and non-immigrant families. Families of West Indian origin were larger and there were slightly more single parents but the nuclear family was found to be the norm. Among cultural characteristics identified as different from non-immigrant families, some were perceived as positive: parents of Caribbean heritage were found to exercise tighter control of their children and encouraged them to be more self-reliant. It was argued that these were qualities which would help children's development but that there was a danger that tighter control might causes conflicts between parents and children as they grew older. The authors' main concerns related to attitudes to play. Informal observations suggested that less importance might be attached to play by families of Caribbean heritage and that this might in turn affect children's development (Rutter et al, 1975).

Thus, articles written in the sixties and seventies on the effect of pupils' homes show clearly that many researchers looked to pupils' families and homes for causes of underachievement. The implicit assumption — wholly unjustifiable — was that these were deficient in many ways. It was also commonly assumed that the problems lay with the child.

Problematising the Child

Problems were perceived in three key areas: intelligence, self- esteem and behaviour.

During the sixties views of fixed intelligence flourished and intelligence testing was the norm. Children of Caribbean heritage frequently scored below average in such tests, because of the cultural bias inherent in tests and problems associated with the background of those implementing the tests (Bagley et al, 1978). Nevertheless, the belief that some groups have an inherently lower level of intelligence became more overt and acceptable, nourished by work by Jensen in America and the publication in Britain in 1969 of Eysenck's *Race, Intelligence and Education.*

Black parents and community groups were particularly concerned that low achievement was being attributed to innate low intelligence. A report on an enquiry into the achievement of pupils of Caribbean heritage in Redbridge said:

We were disturbed to find that on a number of occasions when discussing this Enquiry in the Borough that the names of Jensen and Eysenck were mentioned quite spontaneously by local teachers. Although no teacher admitted to believing in the genetic inferiority of black people, the claim by Professor Arthur Jensen to have shown that negroes were of lower intelligence than whites was clearly close to these teachers' thoughts... The Working Party considered the genetic explanation of underachievement and found that Jensen's views had been completely refuted at an academic level... (Black People's Progressive Association, 1978).

Such views persisted, however, and were discussed, debated and researched. The Committee of Inquiry into the Education of Children from Ethnic Minority Groups commissioned a review of work on IQ. This led to the conclusion in the Swann Report (1985) that the review, carried out by Professor Mackintosh — 'a distinguished psychologist... and his colleague Dr. Mascie-Taylor' had 'disposed of the idea that West Indian underachievement can be explained away by reference to IQ scores' (Department of Education and Science, 1985).

Consequently, innately lower intelligence as a factor became less common in educational debates. Decreased use of intelligence tests and a change in the research focus in examining ethnic minority achievement, to be discussed later in this chapter, may also have contributed to the demise of this aspect of problematising the child. (But see pages 8, 39 on a recent revival of this notion.)

The second debate, which has also become less common, concerns the self-concept of children of Caribbean heritage and the thesis that children are damaged by prejudiced attitudes and discrimination. It was argued that the prevailing view that black people are inferior, and the racist practices based on this view, affect the self-concept of pupils of Caribbean heritage, lowering their 'self-esteem' i.e. the value they place on themselves.

The theory was widely discussed in relation to a publication by Bernard Coard, a teacher from Granada. This book was a polemic focusing on the disproportionate number of West Indian pupils in schools for the educationally sub-normal (ESN schools) and included a chapter on self-concept (Coard, 1971). It was given further credence by research which investigated self-concept through pupils' responses to black and white dolls and concluded that pupils of Caribbean heritage were reluctant to identify with black dolls (Milner, 1975).

Much of the work which followed focused on estimating self-concept, as reviews show (Taylor, 1981). Indeed, low self-esteem seemed to be accepted as a reality and attention focused on measuring its level, while multicultural education was seen as a solution to the 'problem'. Many early initiatives in multicultural education in multiracial schools can be attributed to this interest in increasing the self-concept of children of Caribbean heritage.

Occasionally researchers looked at the link with achievement (Bagley et al, 1979. Driver, 1982). One pioneering study with a very different agenda, that of examining the effect of teachers on different ethnic minority groups, also examined the link. This study started with a theoretical exposition of steps through which achievement might be influenced by a pupil's self-concept (Green, 1985).

The criticisms of the increasing focus on low self-concept took many forms, all of which criticised the tendency of those involved to problematise or pathologise the child. Some argued that pupils of Caribbean heritage had a positive image of themselves, not a negative one. Thus, one detailed study measured the self-concept and achievements of pupils in supplementary schools and concluded that children did not suffer from low self-esteem. It argued that the causes of 'underachievement' lay in the teaching styles in schools. It was said that pupils succeeded in Supplementary Schools and that mainstream teaching styles were not appropriate for pupils of Caribbean heritage (Stone, 1981). Another stressed the danger that with a focus on promoting cultural identity, teachers might concentrate on this rather than on achievement, and might not teach children effectively (Tomlinson, 1983).

Many others focused mainly on 'self-concept'. Some argued that 'self-concept' was multi-faceted, that children might have a generally positive image but feel less secure in certain areas. Sociologists as well as educationalists drew attention to the fact that children are not passive recipients of values and that groups develop their own criteria and credibility through sub-cultural attributes. Some critics focused on the interpretation and implication of the theory of low esteem, arguing that this is misleading, suggesting as it does that the child is not only passive but incomplete, deficient and in need of topping up (Verma, 1990).

Thus, poor self-concept, or in some cases a confusion about identity, was debated at length as a possible cause of 'underachievement'.

Looking at behaviour, it seems clear that black pupils have been regularly perceived as deviant and disruptive. In the early days of immigration, research focused on children referred to child guidance clinics and, for this discrete group, researchers concluded that the separations imposed by immigration were a contributory factor to poor behaviour (Graham and Meadows, 1967).

Later research focused on pupils of Caribbean heritage in schools and examined behaviour as perceived by teachers. In one study of seven year olds in five multiracial schools in London, their teachers' perceptions of their behaviour were measured, using a Rutter Behaviour Questionnaire. In the study, these pupils were perceived as having significant behavioural disorders. This was as true of pupils not affected by separation as those who were. Teacher descriptions of these young pupils included terms like 'squirmy', 'fidgety', 'disliked by others', 'irritable', 'often miserable', 'disobedient', 'attention- seeking' (Bagley, 1972).

The team of researchers previously cited for their examination of the part played by homes, led by Rutter and including Bagley, also examined pupils' behaviour in London schools. Their study was larger than that described in the paragraph above, included parent interviews and focused on ten year olds (Rutter et al, 1974). The research confirmed that teachers saw pupils of Caribbean heritage as proportionately between twice and three times more deviant than the rest of the sample. Restlessness, poor concentration, destructiveness and quarrelsome attitudes were cited and, occasionally for girls, being alone or miserable or fearful. Like the research on pupils' homes, this research raised questions about some of the current perceptions of those of Caribbean heritage. Behavioural difficulties at school *were* more common amongst West Indian children but according to the researchers, West Indian children 'did not differ from other children in terms of disorder shown at home, nor did they differ in terms of emotional disturbance in any setting' (Rutter et al, 1974).

Racism as a Cause

In the very earliest years of concern, some researchers acknowledged that 'prejudice' might be a contributory factor to unequal educational outcomes. But, it was mentioned in passing, most attention being paid to factors problematising the child or the family (see, for example, the review of research by Goldman and Taylor, 1966). Later, in the seventies and early eighties, there were studies demonstrating that teachers stereotyped or had negative views of pupils of Caribbean heritage (see reviews of work done in these years by Taylor (1981), Tomlinson (1983) and Figueroa (1991)). However, the prevailing emphasis continued to be on the child and the family, rather than examining the role of the school.

The black community had a very different approach. While family/child factors might be discussed and examined as factors, racism was seen as highly significant (Black Peoples' Progressive Association and Redbridge Community Relations Council, 1978). Attention focused on the school, and along with poor teaching and low educational standards, racism was considered as a key factor (Tizard et al, 1988).

Concern about achievement and pressure from the Caribbean Community was such that an All Party Select Committee on Race Relations and Immigration recommended in 1977 that an enquiry be carried out to find out if and why lesser achievement occurred. The Committee set up to do this, chaired by Anthony Rampton, produced an interim (Rampton) report in 1981 (Department of Education and Science, 1981). After 1981 Michael Swann took over as Chair and the final (Swann) report was published in 1985 (Department of Education and Science, 1985).

The Interim Report provided, for the first time, a publication on education, with official Central Government backing which used the term 'racism' and considered its nature and effect seriously and at length. As a result, the Report was instrumental in changing the direction of research and of local education authority policy. It validated action by all those who believed that racism existed and was harmful, and it encouraged others to discuss the possibility that thinking about racism and its effects should be on their agenda.

The section in the Report on factors contributing to underachievement began with three pages on racism. These pages began:

> Many West Indians insisted to us that the major reason for the underachievement of their children at school was racism.. and its effects both in schools and in society generally. Many other people who gave evidence to us mentioned racism as a contributory factor.

30

In our view racism describes a set of attitudes and behaviour towards people of another race which is based on the belief that races are distinct and can be graded as 'superior' or 'inferior' (Department of Education and Science, 1981).

The report was careful to point out that negative and patronising or stereotypical views might be held by 'well-intentioned and apparently sympathetic people'. It also distinguished between the 'intentional' racism of a minority of teachers with explicitly racist views, and the more common 'unintentional' racism associated with stereotyped or patronising attitudes. Both types of racism influenced the performance of children of Caribbean heritage. According to the Committee, teachers' behaviour was influenced by attitudes e.g. that West Indian pupils were more difficult, holding low expectations of academic ability, and a 'we treat all children the same' philosophy.

The Committee reported on their findings on 'institutional racism'. The eurocentric nature of the curriculum, of teaching resources, and of exam questions were all identified as important elements, as was the disproportionate allocation to ability based teaching groups, and pastoral care arrangements that were insensitive to ethnic minority needs. Home-school links were said to be poor. Undue numbers of children of Caribbean heritage were placed in schools for the educationally subnormal because tests were culturally biased. Disproportionate suspension of pupils of Caribbean heritage was also considered as a factor contributing to disadvantage but no conclusions were drawn because of the lack of adequate data.

Partly as a result of Rampton, emphasis began to shift from the family and child to the school. Researchers looked at the source and perpetuation of racism and reflected on the nature of racism in schools and on the effectiveness of local education policies slowly being introduced to reduce it.

Much of the research after 1985 did not focus directly on pupils of Caribbean heritage, or indeed on any ethnic minority background. Several factors may have contributed to this change. One was the move to looking at multicultural education for all pupils. This was stressed as a priority in the Final Report of the Committee. The Swann Report considered the effects of teacher racism on achievement, but placed a greater emphasis on the wider problems caused by racism in society (Department of

31

Education and Science, 1985). A second factor was the increased interest in developing strategies for the management of change associated with the need to implement multicultural or antiracist education initiatives.

A third factor was the interminable debates at a theoretical level about the nature and desirability of multicultural as opposed to antiracist education. The latter arose initially because of complaints that 'multicultural education', as manifested in occasional cultural evenings or projects and Black Studies modules, did little to promote the achievement of pupils of Caribbean heritage. But the debates soon took on a rhetoric and momentum of their own.

As time progressed, researchers concentrated also on the taught curriculum. Their priority was the development of subject-specific curricula with a consistent permeation of a multicultural/antiracist philosophy. Sometimes the effects of new initiatives were researched but frequently the focus in this was on white pupils, their attitudes and the extent to which these might be changed. Researchers did not look at the effects on the achievement of pupils of Caribbean heritage, for there was a tendency to take it for granted that the traditional and eurocentric curriculum was racist and associated with a poor self-concept of pupils of Caribbean heritage whereas the new curriculum would promote their achievement.

While publications since 1981 focused primarily on policy, the management of change, and improving the taught curriculum, a few carried out studies with more immediate implications for racism and for ethnic minority pupils including those of Caribbean heritage.

One, based on work carried out in the seventies, was published in the Swann Report. This was pioneering work by an author who argued for the need to find out about the: 'dynamics of teaching' and to lift the 'veil of obscurity which inevitably conceals much of any teacher's work' in examining outcomes for ethnic minority pupils. This study was located therefore in classrooms. It employed a Flanders schedule to enable a systematic and statistical investigation of the nature and effects of teacher-pupil interaction to be made (Green, 1985).

Green was interested in the effect of teachers and sought to examine this by using a large scale study with many teachers, thus ensuring that they covered a range of philosophies and teaching styles. In all, there were seventy teachers in six schools, situated in two local authorities and including some middle and some junior schools. In the teachers' classes were nearly 2000 pupils, including about 500 pupils of Asian origin and about 300 of Caribbean heritage.

Teachers who had been identified by questionnaire as less 'ethnically tolerant' than others, used a teaching style which was less responsive to pupils generally and especially so for ethnic minority pupils. They used less questioning and more direct teaching, took less notice of ethnic minority pupils' ideas and feelings, and gave them less opportunities for initiatory talk. This was especially true for pupils of Caribbean heritage, and, in some cases, girls were more excluded than boys.

Ethnographic and Other Research on Racism since the Mid-Eighties

Since the mid-eighties, other researchers have worked in classrooms using an essentially ethnographic method for doing their research. This is partly because of the absence of work on pupils' feelings about racism and about teacher attitudes. A more open-ended approach enabled researchers to focus on pupils' experiences and to try to identify the processes through which racism affected them. Their work, like that of the Swann Committee, indicated that there were teachers with racist or intolerant views and that pupils of Caribbean heritage in their classes were treated differently.

The earliest study based on the ethnographic approach was situated in fourth and fifth forms in two multiracial comprehensives. Observations by Wright suggested that there were problems in relationships between some teachers and pupils, revealing hostility on the part of the teacher. From comments made by teachers and conversations with pupils, the researcher argued that the poor quality of relationships derived primarily from negative teacher attitudes towards pupils of Caribbean heritage. She asserted that teacher attitudes influenced the placement of these pupils in ability sets and, hence, were responsible for their disproportionate allocation to lower ability sets (Wright, 1985).

Also using an ethnographic approach, Gillborn carried out a two year study of boys in one year group in a multiracial school in the nineteen eighties. He combined observations in classrooms with the collation and analysis of data on disciplinary incidents and argued that teachers were more critical of boys of Caribbean heritage and reprimands were more likely for these pupils than other pupils who behaved in similar ways (Gillborn, 1990).

Records on discipline showed that teachers gave vague reasons for detention of pupils of Afro-Caribbean heritage, citing rudeness or being a nuisance on the stairs, rather than breaking specific school rules, as they did for detention of other pupils. Records confirmed that pupils of Caribbean heritage were sanctioned more frequently than others and that sanctions were more severe for identical offences. Of children of Afro-Caribbean heritage 68% received detentions compared with 31% of white children and about half of pupils of Asian background (Gillborn, 1990).

A third study was based on a year spent in two inner city schools in the early eighties. Using the information gained about teachers from conversations and observation in classrooms, and a good deal of information about female pupils from observation and interviews, Mirza argued that girls of Caribbean heritage were disadvantaged because teachers assessed their abilities incorrectly. Overt and unintentional racism underlay teacher attitudes and affected the choice of subjects studied by these pupils, their placement in teaching groups, and the comparatively poorer advice and guidance they received about possible opportunities available when they left school (Mirza, 1992).

While many studies employed ethnographic methodology, supplementing and testing observations with other data, Brook's study involved a systematic and statistical analysis of the interaction of seven teachers with year seven pupils in a secondary school. The researcher adapted and used the Optic Observation method. It was found that there were differences in the treatment of pupils of Caribbean heritage compared with others and that these were statistically significant. Pupils of Caribbean heritage received proportionately more negative comments than other pupils, comments which were primarily associated with negative behaviour (Brook, 1991).

As well as looking at the effects of teachers and their responses to pupils, these studies examined the reactions of pupils of Caribbean heritage to their experiences in the classroom. Pupils faced with unfair treatment were not passive about this. Wright reported that students were angry and hostile towards those concerned (Wright, 1985). Gillborn suggested that while some boys rebelled at the treatment received, others developed strategies of 'accommodation' to minimise the disadvantages they faced (Gillborn, 1990). Mirza suggested that, rather than rebelling, many girls persisted in a determined effort to succeed academically, using coping strategies to avoid problems and keep away from less tolerant teachers, trying to work effectively and make the best choices possible to achieve academically despite their disadvantaged situation (Mirza, 1992).

The studies also threw some light on the different experiences of pupils of Caribbean heritage compared with those who originated from the Asian sub-continent. Teaching styles were more negative for the former and they attracted more criticism and more sanctioning for similar behaviour (Green, 1985. Gillborn, 1990. Brook, 1991). This conclusion should not be interpreted as suggesting that pupils from families originating from Asia enjoy equal opportunities for, even if teacher attitudes towards this group of ethnic minority pupils are less intentionally racist, other effects of racism may disadvantage them in comparison with white pupils (Hyder, 1993). Nevertheless, it appears that pupils of Caribbean heritage experience greater and more overt hostility from some teachers and are, in effect, even more 'vulnerable' than pupils originating from the Asian sub-continent.

The research, then, shows that negative teacher attitudes can be a contributory and harmful factor in the school experiences of pupils of Caribbean heritage, with pupils suffering from a poorer quality of relations due to the 'gut' responses of teachers and their perceptions of pupil behaviour. Not all studies use the term 'racist' but most indicate relations in which teachers were more hostile and critical and curtailed opportunities for pupils. The research also suggests that low teacher expectation contributes to disadvantage and that school structures reflect and perpetuate it and may reinforce stereotypes. The structures identified encompass subject groupings, allocation to ability groups and sanctions such as suspensions for poor behaviour. In short, the conclusions of the Rampton Report in 1981 appear to be confirmed by this body of research.

Schools as a Cause

The most recent debate centres on the view that the poor quality of the schools attended explains the lesser achievement of pupils of Caribbean heritage. Underlying this is the assumption that pupils of Caribbean heritage are concentrated in inner cities schools and that a relatively large proportion of the schools are 'ineffective' and have lower educational standards.

Support for this comes from a quantitative study published in 1989 (Smith and Tomlinson, 1989). This key study received considerable media attention. Its conclusions about ethnic minority pupils have since been criticised because of its methodological and interpretative problems (Gillborn, 1990). Nevertheless it is still quoted by many as evidence that ineffective schools are the cause of underachievement.

Planning for the research began in 1980 in a context of great concern about the perpetuation of unequal educational outcomes for ethnic minority pupils and, at the same time, of increasing interest in differences in school effectiveness. The central objective was to adjust the academic outcomes obtained in a sample of secondary schools for pupils' attainment at entry to the school, with a view to comparing schools' academic outcomes overall and for different minority groups.

The study by Smith and Tomlinson was sophisticated and impressive. It followed a large group of pupils, 3000 in all at the beginning of the research in 1981, from their transfer to secondary school to the end of their fifth year in 1986 when they sat their GCE and CSE examinations. At the start of the research, twenty secondary schools in four areas were involved. The research employed new and complex statistical methodology, called multi-level analysis, developed from regression techniques. This enabled the researchers to use longitudinal data for individual pupils, i.e. data collected in different years, and to analyse pupils' examination results in the light of their previous achievement and of the differences in educational achievement which may exist between schools.

Some of the important issues, and discussions about them, were not easily and quickly accessible. The book was long — over three hundred pages. Some chapters were difficult to absorb because of the detail and quantitative material presented. There was no index to help the reader to select and cross-reference.

Not surprisingly, many have read only the conclusions publicised in the media. One point sometimes glossed over in media reports was that its focus on the effectiveness of schools meant that the study was interested in progress rather than absolute levels of achievement. The focus on progress is clear in the authors' accounts and also in an article by one of the authors written the following year:

There are considerable differences between urban comprehensive schools in the levels of attainment reached by pupils with similar background characteristics and initial attainments'... the 'same child' might get a CSE grade 3 in one school and an' O-level grade B' in another (Tomlinson, 1990).

Three conclusions from the book were quoted frequently in the press and are particularly relevant here. One relates to the relevance of ethnicity, a second to the position of ethnic minorities vis-a-vis the majority group, and the third to implications of 'race' and background. The relevant passages from the concluding chapter are these:

The differences in exam results attributable to ethnic group are very much smaller than those attributable to the school. In other words, what school a child goes to makes far more difference (in terms of exam results) than what ethnic group he or she belongs to...

...some schools are much better than others, and the ones that are good for white people tend to be about equally good for black people...

there is no evidence that racial hostility is at school an important factor for twelve and thirteen year old children... school effectiveness is an issue for racial minorities in much the same way as it is for everyone else... this does not mean that racial and cultural differences have no importance in secondary education... children tend strongly to choose friends from the same sex and from among their own racial group... schools vary substantially in the extent to which friendships cross racial boundaries (Smith and Tomlinson, 1989).

The implications were that schools were the cause of lesser achievement, that ethnicity was irrelevant and that problems faced by ethnic minorities were similar to those of all pupils and, finally, that racism is not an issue though race and background are relevant in so far as they influence interpersonal interaction through friendship patterns. Thus, the conclusion of this study paints quite a different picture to that given by the researchers above.

Smith and Tomlinson were unable to examine why differences between schools occur. One report which looked at seven urban areas characterised by high levels of social and economic disadvantage, indicated problem areas which can occur in some schools. These include curriculum planning which neglects the needs due to children's disadvantaged backgrounds and pays insufficient attention to raising achievement. Poor teaching may be a problem, with unskilled teaching in communication skills, and unchallenging and unmotivating teaching across the curriculum. Schools may underestimate pupils' abilities. Managers may fail to set standards or ensure that learning is monitored and evaluated (see Department for Education, 1993c).

The view that poor schooling explains underachievement by children of Caribbean heritage has been a very powerful one, not least because it is held by people with a range of perspectives. It appeals to those who believe that the problems of ethnic minority pupils are no different to the difficulties which may be experienced by white pupils and that multicultural or antiracist education is not only unnecessary but even detrimental to the delivery of education. The latter is not consistent with the views of Smith and Tomlinson who argued that it is important for schools to reflect the multicultural society in which we live. Unfortunately the need for adopting a multicultural philosophy was not considered in any detail in their analysis and, in any case, their concluding sentences on the need for multicultural education received little attention. That schools are the cause of unequal outcomes may equally be believed by supporters of multicultural or antiracist education.

Attributing poor attainment to the quality of schooling is also supported by many parents of Caribbean heritage, who have argued for decades that — along with racism — poor standards in schools are the cause of underachievement. They attack more progressive teaching styles or the extent to which a preoccupation with multicultural education to improve self-esteem has taken attention away from improving teaching (Stone, 1981).

So, groups with very different views on the education of pupils of Caribbean heritage may all appear to subscribe to the 'schools are the cause' theory of underachievement.

Deficit Theories, Different Perspectives

We have observed the three theories used to explain the lesser achievement of pupils of Caribbean heritage. The first, which looked at the pupils and their homes, has dwindled since the publication of the Rampton Report but still has an impact. It underlies some teachers' responses, may occur in research (e.g. Dawson, 1988) and has resurfaced explicitly in a recent publication about IQ tests (Herrnstein and Murray, 1994).The second theory, focusing on racism as a cause, has continued to be influential, although the term 'racism' is often avoided. The third theory, focusing on schools, has gained ascendancy since Smith and Tomlinson's study of 1989. Some people who previously emphasised strategies based on the 'racism is the cause' theory may now give greater emphasis to improving schools.

All three theories have been subject to attack and criticism and to considerable debate. As indicated earlier, some criticisms of the first concentrated on specific variables in the theory itself. But there was a far more fundamental criticism of it, which centred on the extent to which the theory problematised or pathologised the child and family (See inter alia Wright, 1987; Troyna, 1990; Figueroa, 1991.) On the one hand, said these and other critics, it ignored the effect of racism and the part played by schools in causing underachievement and on the other hand, it omitted any consideration of positive attributes of those of Caribbean heritage and ignored the achievements of the pupils of Caribbean heritage who did manage to succeed academically.

Criticisms of the second theory have targeted the methodology used by researchers and also the apparent omission of research on pupils of Caribbean heritage located in schools with teachers who are not racist (Foster, 1990). Criticisms of the the the third theory focused on the study of school effectiveness itself rather than on the underlying theory. Critics drew attention to a range of problems within the study, including its design and the omission of qualitative analysis to clarify the role of racism (Gillborn,1990).

When one looks at the many decades of research and discussions on the lesser achievement of pupils of Caribbean heritage, it is clear that the debate on causal factors has been a stormy one. The different experiences, interests and personal experiences and backgrounds of those involved, whether in the academic or the wider community, make this almost inevitable. Frequently, research challenging the 'family causes' theory was carried out by, or arose because of links with members of the Caribbean community or others with 'political' interests. Responses to the second theory that racism is the cause of underachievement were angry and sometimes defensive.

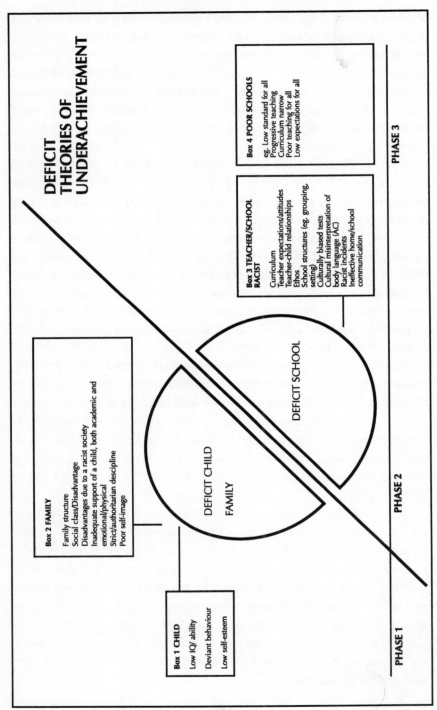

DEFICIT
THEORIES OF
UNDERACHIEVEMENT

Box 2 FAMILY
Family structure
Social class/Disadvantage
Disadvantages due to a racist society
Inadequate support of a child, both academic and
emotional/physical
Strict/authoritarian descipline
Poor self-image

Box 1 CHILD
Low IQ/ ability
Deviant behaviour
Low self-esteem

DEFICIT CHILD
FAMILY

DEFICIT SCHOOL

**Box 3 TEACHER/SCHOOL
RACIST**
Curriculum
Teacher expectations/attitudes
Teacher-child relationships
Ethos
School structures (eg. grouping,
setting)
Culturally biased tests
Cultural misinterpretation of
body language (AC)
Racist incidents
Ineffective home/school
communication

Box 4 POOR SCHOOLS
eg. Low standard for all
Progressive teaching
Curriculum narrow
Poor teaching for all
Low expectations for all

PHASE 1   PHASE 2   PHASE 3

The debate inevitably involved issues beyond the purely intellectual. As one author has argued, frames of reference involving different races and ethnic groups have evaluative and affective aspects as well as cognitive ones (Figueroa, 1991). Not surprisingly, there are issues which are difficult to discuss objectively.

Factors included in the three theories are summarised in the tables opposite. Possibly as a result of the nature of the debate and the issues involved, the theories are all deficit theories and the people supporting them tended to attribute blame to individuals or groups and to 'problematise' those involved. Only factors seen as acting negatively were discussed. The 'deficit' approach of the first theory neglects high achievers among pupils of Caribbean heritage. The positive contributions of parents and pupils are omitted by those pathologising pupils and homes. Antiracist or more positive teachers and the high achieving schools with pupils of Caribbean heritage are ignored by those who follow the second theory and problematise the schools. The third theory, especially in its earliest days, disregarded the successes of good inner city schools.

The deficit approach and the emotively charged nature of debate in this area may help explain why we still have no clear and consistent answers to the causes of lesser achievement and strategies to resolve it. Moreover, the progress of research and perceptions of the factors involved has been strongly influenced by other debates, to which we now briefly turn.

Other Debates

Some have their origin in research ideas in the States. Some have been partly sociological, to do with class and gender. Others have been primarily to do with education. Changing perspectives on the role of schools have been particularly important. Some controversies involving psychologists have played a part, the most publicised being those about whether intelligence is fixed and the relative influences of nature and nurture. Other discussions have involved political scientists, as for example those to do with laws, the political climate and attitudes to race, and those focusing on ethnic and, more recently, national 'identity'. Research and discussions by sociologists on social class, educationalists' views on the role of schools, and approaches to gender issues have the most immediate relevance to the progress of theories of achievement.

The interest in social class in the nineteen sixties, and especially in the consequences of being 'working class' explains the early preoccupation with the social class of pupils of Caribbean heritage, as discussed in chapter 1. It is partly responsible for the dismissal of lesser achievement as an ethnicity issue by some, a response to ethnic minority underachievement which has persisted for forty years. In effect, it has drawn attention away from issues associated with race and discrimination and, moreover, has contributed to the inattention to the specific characteristics of the 'working class' of Caribbean heritage. For as we saw, values, expectations and responsibilities within families of Caribbean heritage can differ from those of the white population and the educational consequences of being white and working class may therefore differ from those of being working class and of Caribbean heritage.

In addition, the development of ideas on class have played an important part in the path taken by the achievement debate. Some aspects of this were well documented in an article in *Multiracial Education* in 1983 (Reeves and Chevannes, 1983), which argued that the poor self-concept explanation of underachievement, common in the seventies and eighties, was linked with theories of 'cultural deficit', the 'cultural deprivation' of those of 'lower social class'. Increasing concern about the patronising approach inherent in the concept of 'cultural deficit' and in its incorrect assumptions about the 'lower classes' led eventually to the rejection of these theories.

The criticising of the low self-concept theory was part of this phase and, like 'cultural deficit' theories, gave way to theories of disadvantage. Moreover, with the falling into disrepute in the seventies of cultural deficit theories generally, 'blaming' homes and pupils became less acceptable. The earliest deficit theory, that the underachievement of pupils of Caribbean heritage was associated with families and pupils, became less acceptable.

The focus in socio-political discussions on class moved on to 'disadvantage', including educational disadvantage. In the eighties, this approach was criticised for ignoring the perspective of the groups involved. There was a shift to examining the responses of 'powerless' groups. The ethnographic methodology was developed and it was argued from the research which followed that powerless groups were not passive acceptors of their position in society but developed their own sub-cultures and indicators of 'success'. Educational research on people of Caribbean heritage, who were perceived by many as powerless, reflected this trend. While the research was useful, the new focus was on group behaviour and aspirations. Hence achievement and the factors associated with it became secondary considerations or even irrelevant.

The development of theories on ethnic minority achievement has also been influenced by changing educational philosophies about the role of schools. Considerations of school factors in the second deficit theory was facilitated by the increasing interest in the influence of schools' differences in school effectiveness and factors responsible for it (Rutter, 1979. Mortimore, 1988).

The third and latest deficit theory of 'poor schools as a cause' moved research directly in line with general research on school effectiveness. This may partly have reflected the sharper focusing on the role of schools as efficient/inefficient institutions, precipitated by the Education Reform Act and its perception of schools as institutions producing a consumer 'free market' product. The consequences were that less priority was given to the individual pupil or groups of pupils. Considerations of equality of opportunity gave way to criteria based on cost effectiveness, the economic/market approach to education, and an abstract individualistic conception of the pupil (Troyna, 1991). The third deficit theory was part of this trend.

Research on the effect of gender on achievement seemed to show girls of Caribbean heritage in some cases performing better than boys (see chapter 1). Previous developments by some sociologists, often unjustifiably pathologising black families and especially adult males, led increasingly to perceptions of the 'strong black woman', thus rationalising the theory of female achievement.

The interest in gender issues in education accelerated, propelled by the growth in gender studies and interest in the life experiences of women generally. With this, ethnographic research, located in schools and focusing on ethnic minority pupils, examined the specific and potentially different experiences of girls and boys and provided useful insight into the educational experiences of pupils of Caribbean background (Mac an Ghail, 1988. Gillborn, 1990. Mirza, 1992).

However, educational research on young women of Caribbean heritage excluded and misrepresented achievement issues, and the potential underachievement of girls was ignored. Interest in the achievement of pupils of Caribbean heritage concentrated exclusively on boys, and progress in the understanding of the effect of children's backgrounds on their achievement slowed down as a result.

While developments in Sociology and Education have influenced the course of the debate on achievement, attitudes to discussions about racism, its prevalence and its effects have in turn shaped discussions on race and education. Political changes and the influence of key politicians in recent years have been well documented (Troyna and Hatcher, 1991. Gillborn, 1993) and may well have contributed to the fact that research on racism and its effects has become rather limited.

Clearly, then, it is important to consider other ongoing debates and research interests when looking at why the achievement debate has progressed as it has. Other priorities in research have been influential in affecting changes in the areas researched. In some cases they have caused ethnic minority issues to be treated as part of a more general issue; in others they have drawn attention from the main debate about the achievement of ethnic minority students.

Methodology

In the earliest years of the debate, conclusions from the ongoing quantitative research were often questioned on the grounds that many studies were too small to justify generalising from research at the time. One reviewer classified studies according to whether they were large-scale, medium-scale or small-scale, and concluded that:

> there are enough large-scale studies using total samples of over 600 children to counter charges that the research is small-scale and biased (Tomlinson, 1983).

Quantitative studies have also been criticised for sampling and design problems and not adequately explaining why ethnic minorities achieve less well. For example, an article published in 1991 evaluated the strengths and weaknesses of ten key quantitative studies of examination results. The authors concluded that:

> to date, we lack a study with a sufficient number of pupils and schools, covering a sufficient range of variables, with a nationally repre-

sentative sample, combining both qualitative and quantitative data gathering (Drew and Gray, 1991).

Another article focused on two recent studies and highlighted their inadequacies (Gillborn, 1990). One was an examination of external examination results from a 'youth cohort' study, a national study involving a sample of about 14,000 young people including 700 ethnic minority students who reached minimum school-leaving age in the summer of 1985 and who were followed up by postal questionnaires on three occasions (Drew and Gray, 1990). The second was the multi-level analysis already described in this chapter which started with 3000 students in their first year of secondary schooling in 1981. The study analysed the 1986 examination results of 2,500 of these students including about 950 pupils of ethnic minority origin (Smith and Tomlinson, 1989).

Because race, class and gender effects in the youth cohort study explained only ten per cent of differences in achievement, Gillborn examined the multi-level analysis of school effectiveness critically and at length, to clarify whether the effect of the school attended was the crucial missing factor. The difficulties experienced in the latter study and its deficiencies were such that he concluded that it was 'only a first step in a field which has few certainties and many confusions'. He went on to justify ethnographic methodology, arguing that in view of the complexity of life in multi-ethnic schools, quantitative research needed to be complemented by qualitative research on processes and pupils' school experiences (Gillborn, 1990).

With the inadequate conclusions about cause and, more importantly, the need to clarify processes, researchers turned to qualitative techniques, spending long periods in schools and with young people outside schools, and collecting qualitative data to analyse their experiences and the effect of teacher attitudes. This genre of research has been considered briefly in this chapter but will be analysed at length in chapter 8. As will be seen, there have been methodological debates, just as for the quantitative studies. Some critics have argued that qualitative studies may have serious methodological weaknesses and biases and that conclusions may be drawn, unjustifiably, from very small and atypical samples (Foster, 1990). Others have been critical about the design of research, arguing that in some studies this may be biased and influenced by the perspective of the researcher (Connolly, 1992).

The debates about methodology, whether quantitative or qualitative, have increased the difficulties of drawing conclusions about the causes of unequal outcomes. This is not to say that the debates are unnecessary. To take one example, recurring and important issues have been the size of a study and how classrooms are sampled, important considerations in qualitative studies, as will be seen in chapter 8. It is also relevant in quantitative studies, even the more large-scale.

Thus, for example, in the work by Smith and Tomlinson, quoted by many who support the 'schools as the cause' theory, conclusions about pupils of Caribbean heritage can be questioned. The relatively small number of pupils of Caribbean heritage, 146 in total, and the very small numbers in individual schools, makes it difficult to test the significance of within-school differences in the achievement of pupils of Caribbean heritage relative to others in the same school. Thus, the relative importance of within-school and between-school factors can scarcely be established, although the researchers claim to have done so. Moreover, the sample of schools involved was far from representative of schools in society, and the size of the sample small in relation to the numbers of students of Caribbean heritage at school in Britain and doing exams in 1986. It is not justifiable therefore to extrapolate from the study and draw conclusions about pupils of Caribbean heritage in Britain. This study sheds little light on the extent to which underachievement arises because of a concentration of pupils of Caribbean heritage in inner city schools which are less successful.

In short, criticisms and counter-criticisms about methodology have helped to complicate and confuse the achievement debate. It is, of course important to reflect on methodology, as is done in chapters 8 and 9. But the debates and the underlying methodological problems have added to the difficulty of clarifying the key causes of underachievement.

Achievement and its Causes Revisited

This chapter suggests that research theories on the lesser achievement of pupils of Caribbean heritage have been strongly influenced by the perspectives and experiences of those involved. Additionally, other research agendas and trends plus methodological problems, have inhibited the formation of firm and consistent conclusions thirty years on.

There has been some progress, however. Research has moved on since the earliest theory focused on families and pupils. The dust has settled, there is greater knowledge and understanding about the families concerned, and some of the irrelevant variables have been rejected. With the second theory, focusing on teacher attitudes and racism, it is accepted that these might play a part in unequal outcomes. Moreover, there have been improvements and changes in research methodology, with the development of a qualitative approach which helps the understanding of the processes and effects of teacher attitudes, and with the progression from simple correlation analysis in quantitative research to covariance analysis and, more recently, multi-level analysis.

Nevertheless, the effect of differences in perspectives and the consequent consistent use of a deficit or problem approach, has left its legacy. The problem approach continues to be a barrier to increasing understanding of pupils' progress and achievement.

The dichotomy of research and researchers into the problematising of the child/family, the problematising of teachers and the problematising of schools, also has repercussions and implications for fostering achievement. It predicates against a genuine consideration of any negative factors associated with pupils if the focus is on the harmful effects of teachers. For example, pupils may rebel against teachers in situations of hostility and improvement strategies depend crucially on changing teacher attitudes or, at the very least, their actions. But equally one ought to be considering what should be done directly to promote more acceptable pupil behaviour, rather than giving the message that such behaviour can be condoned.

In short, it could be argued that while new theories have redressed some of the shortcomings of earlier theories, these initiatives are unbalanced and incomplete. It is time to develop a new approach — one that incorporates racism but treats it as one of several factors in a complex theory which can explain both underachievement and achievement.

Chapter 3

Research Design and Background

Chapters 3 to 7 describe new research that I carried out in 1992. I designed it in light of my belief that the decades of study have given us no clear guidance about the achievement of pupils of Caribbean heritage and how to promote it. As someone from the Caribbean, where there are high achievers, and as a teacher who has both worked in a Saturday School and developed and coordinated a Section 11 Project to increase the achievement of pupils of Caribbean background, I could see that more research was required.

Recently published studies located in the classroom focus almost exclusively on racist or 'less aware' teachers. This does not seem realistic or balanced in the nineteen nineties when schools in England, and their teachers, can be expected to hold a wide range of attitudes to racial and cultural differences, with racist schools at one extreme and, at the other, schools where some teachers are aware of and interested in ethnic minority needs. My research aimed to restore the balance by specifically locating a study in schools thought to be closer to the 'more aware' end of the spectrum.

Location of the Research

The five chapters are based on data collected while based in schools in the Spring and Autumn Terms of 1992. Two authorities in the Midlands were chosen for the research, one a metropolitan authority and the other a county authority. The research uses a purposive sample of schools perceived by specialist advisory staff and advisers in these authorities as being more 'positive' i.e genuinely interested in ensuring that equal opportunities are available for their black pupils.

Other criteria considered and discussed with advisory staff were that the sample of schools should ideally include some with black teachers or headteachers, and that there should be schools with relatively large numbers of pupils of Caribbean heritage and with relatively few. As most of the research on pupils' experiences to date has been located in secondary schools and as, according to Maxime, children in the age group seven to twelve are the most sensitive to racial issues, it seemed potentially useful to examine the primary phase of schooling (Maxime, 1986).

The study was located in classrooms with year two pupils. At the time of the research, teachers were carrying out the Standard Assessment Tasks for seven year olds (year two pupils), as required by the 1988 Education Reform Act. It was thought that the levels of attainment obtained from these Tasks for the three core subjects in the National Curriculum would provide a useful and objective measure of pupil achievement and, moreover, that as teachers of these pupils might be focusing more sharply on pupil attainment and the factors associated with it, a study of this year group would be especially helpful.

Four schools were identified for the research. The schools were visited, the research discussed, and the implications of spending time in classes considered by the headteachers. One classteacher was involved in each of three schools and two class teachers in the fourth. The headteachers and all five teachers were agreeable to my being with the classes for the long periods of time involved. I was to spend half a day to a day weekly in each class during the Spring and Autumn Terms so that I could become well acquainted with the classes and pupils and collect a range of data.

Schools

In three schools the headteachers had been quite recently appointed and were keen to develop their school to ensure that there were equal opportunities for different groups of children, and there had been staff training sessions on equal opportunities. These heads were all familiar with aspects of Caribbean culture, had had contact with pupils of Caribbean heritage, and one was originally from the Caribbean.

One of these three schools was medium-sized with about 150 pupils, forty percent of whom had Pakistani or Caribbean or, in a few cases, Bangladeshi backgrounds. Approximately seventeen percent in all were of Caribbean heritage and the school was highly regarded by the parents who respected the head, praised the good relations with parents and valued the assemblies which sometimes had multicultural themes.

The second school was larger, with ten classes of about thirty pupils each, and a nursery. The head was of Caribbean heritage and two other members of staff and a classroom assistant were of Asian background. Seventy-five percent of pupils were of ethnic minority origin, nearly half of them Caribbean. There were prominent displays around the school reflecting pupils' multi-ethnic backgrounds, focusing on such topics as Martin Luther King, black people in Britain and Rastafarianism — a product of the gradual development of the taught curriculum to include ethnic minority figures and perspectives. There were significant inputs on equal opportunities in staff training and school documents were permeated with an equal opportunities philosophy.

The third school had the greatest proportion of ethnic minority pupils, predominantly of Caribbean heritage, and the largest number of pupils on its school rolls. It had sixteen classes and a nursery. One teacher and a nursery nurse were of Caribbean heritage. The school prioritised increasing the multicultural nature of the curriculum to build on children's ethnic backgrounds. Assemblies, projects within the taught curriculum and displays about the school all reflected this approach.

The fourth school was a small Catholic school. It had very few children of ethnic minority origin and almost all were of Caribbean heritage. The six staff included a black teacher and the school's interest in equal opportunities appeared to be due to the commitment of this teacher to raising issues amongst the staff. The staff had had some training in equal opportunities and there were books in the rest of the school and occasional displays reflecting Britain's multicultural nature.

Classrooms and Pupils

Five classes were chosen for the study, containing forty-five pupils of Caribbean heritage in all. The ethnic composition of each class reflected that of the school.

In the two schools with relatively fewer children of Caribbean heritage, the three classes involved included fourteen pupils from families originating from the Caribbean. As two of them transferred to another class in the course of the research, only twelve were included in the study. These three classes were vertically grouped and consisted of year two and year three pupils, and four of the twelve were year three.

The other two classes had many more pupils of Caribbean heritage, thirty-one in all and all were year two. As it would have been difficult to include thirty-one pupils in field work focusing on two classes, thirteen of the thirty-one were chosen for detailed study. The selection was made with the class teachers, to include pupils achieving different degrees of success, to represent as far as possible the variety of successes, strengths and problems perceived amongst pupils of Caribbean heritage, and to include both boys and girls.

Thus twenty-five pupils of Caribbean heritage were identified for detailed study, twenty-one in year two and four in year three.

The Gender of Teachers and Pupils

Four of the five teachers were female. Fourteen of the twenty-five pupils were girls and eleven were boys. The gender of individual teachers and pupils is not revealed in the description of the research as with such small numbers, this helps to increase confidentiality. Frequently the use of a personal pronouns is avoided by writing about 'the teacher' or 'the child'. Where a personal pronoun is used, 'he/his' is used for teachers and 'she/her' for pupils.

'Race' and Background

One might expect children's rich Caribbean heritage to be valued and an asset in their classroom learning experiences. However, it is also possible that this group of children may have hurtful or unsatisfactory classroom experiences because they are black and of Caribbean heritage. They may suffer because of racial hostility or discrimination based on others' perceptions of their 'race' and ethnicity as inferior. There may be problems because of teachers' lack of knowledge about cultural backgrounds which, for some children, may differ from those familiar to the teachers.

The research aimed to examine the ways, if any, in which the classroom experiences of young children of Caribbean heritage differ from those of white pupils, whether positively or negatively. For want of an adequate phrase to describe this, the chapters will refer to experiences arising from 'race' and background'.

The field research was designed to explore four basic questions :

i) What factors affect the achievement/underachievement of pupils of Caribbean heritage?

ii) What classroom models of teaching are there which aim to promote the achievement of pupils of Caribbean heritage?

iii) What messages are children in this group in these classrooms receiving about their 'race' and heritage?

iv) How are the experiences of a child of Caribbean background and her/his achievement influenced by 'race' and heritage?

The Research Methodology

Classroom research can make use of many different methodologies and types of data (Hopkins, 1985. Also see chapter 3 in Conner, 1991). A primarily qualitative approach was chosen for this study, because of the focus on examining the processes through which children's classroom experiences are affected, and its objective of identifying variables which influence achievement. A qualitative approach using qualitative data collected over a period of time can be used for this purpose, whereas a quantitative approach cannot.

Case studies were developed for the pupils selected for detailed study. Achievement and what affects it is a complex matter, and the case study methodology has the advantage of providing valuable insight through an in-depth and intensive investigation in which the 'multifarious phenonema' involved can be explored and analysed (Cohen and Manion, 1989).

As will be seen, a rich range of data were accumulated using different techniques and sources, and the conclusions from these depended on the use of logical inference to identify underlying patterns, as is normal with a case study approach (Mitchell, 1983).

The collection of data by classroom observation and its processing drew from the ethnographic tradition of 'grounding theory', in which observations and a search for patterns lead to a 'plausible story', grounded in the data collected (Burgess, 1985. Delamont, 1992. Hammersley and Atkinson, 1983). Observations were open-ended, recording anything that seemed of interest, with additional and more focused observation where it appeared warranted, and an immersion in notes and transcripts until a picture began to emerge (Edwards and Furlong, 1985).

However, the context in which these open-ended observations were made was influenced by my knowledge and experience of classrooms, and my personal experience. It would be impossible to do research with a completely blank mind. But every attempt was made to be constantly open to new ideas and to alternative interpretations of the patterns emerging.

When making classroom observations, the researcher can function as a participant or a non-participant. I attempted to participate and to be a normal part of the classroom setting, rather than a 'fly on the wall', but I generally tried not to disturb or influence events, empathising with the children and their experiences and also with teachers.

There are difficulties in doing this sort of research. Given the potential for differences in perspective in this research area, 'triangulation' (i.e. the obtaining of information from different sources) is particularly advisable. There is a need to be systematic enough to avoid using isolated features as evidence. There may be multiple interpretations of a single incident so it is important to consistently seek different explanations. In recording, it is essential to make notes of the context, of who and what was involved, and how the situation developed. As will be seen below and in the chapters which follow, I did my best to try to minimise potential difficulties.

Collecting the Data

The qualitative data were collected during the Spring and Summer Terms of 1992. There were two phases in the field research. The second and third questions set out in the section on 'Race' and Background, were explored first in phase one, when observations focused on the whole class and were guided by two general principles: getting to know the classroom and paying special attention to every occasion on which 'race' and background appeared to impinge on teacher activities or children's experiences.

During phase one, time in the classroom was spent circulating among the groups of pupils, focusing on the tasks they were doing, and on their interaction with the teacher and other pupils. Teacher activities observed included teaching and assessment, with the latter covering a large and representative sample of SATS. Whole class 'carpet' sessions were observed and, when possible, the arrival of pupils in the morning and their departure or collection by parents or others after school. Observations were recorded in detail in diary form and kept in a folder for each class.

In the first few weeks, observations were completely open-ended and unstructured. They were reviewed weekly for any patterns which appeared to be emerging, about the classroom environment generally and about the implications for ethnic minority children. In the second part of phase one, I regularly used a schedule I devised in 1991 of all possible teacher activities as a checklist to ensure that no crucial aspects of classroom life were being neglected in the observations. There were also focused investigations of aspects thought by previous researchers to be relevant to ethnic minority pupils' welfare.

Phase two of the field work aimed to explore the first and last questions. The focus was individual pupils rather than the whole class. Observations were organised systematically to ensure that an equal amount of time was spent on each child in the case studies and that a range of activities was covered. Every attempt was made to keep detailed and accurate accounts. Points were jotted down in the classroom and tidied and expanded after school each day.

This phase used a more interactionist ethnographic approach. Case studies were developed for each of the twenty-five pupils of Caribbean heritage identified for detailed research. These children were observed in a number of different situations. The main location was the classroom, where observation sessions varied in focus and scope, covering a range of academic areas, and looking at the case study pupils working individually, in groups, and in whole class activities. I also attended some year and school assemblies at which the class was present and pupils were shadowed in the playground and at dinner. Detailed records were kept of all observations.

These data were complemented by background information, obtained from the children's records and from other teachers who knew the child or their family. When it was possible to talk with parents collecting or bringing children to school, I did so. In addition, children were interviewed twice using a semi-structured and informal approach. The first interview discussed friends, school and home and took place at the beginning of phase two of the research. It was designed to begin building a picture of each child. The second interview, half way through phase two, explored 'race' and background issues. There were also frequent informal and unstructured discussions with pupils and sometimes these were useful in extending or clarifying the analysis.

Gradually, over the period of time spent in schools, a picture was built up of each pupil. The process used to do this, similar to that in the ethnographic approach, involved a continual cyclical reviewing of the emerging picture in the light of fresh evidence, as shown in the diagram:

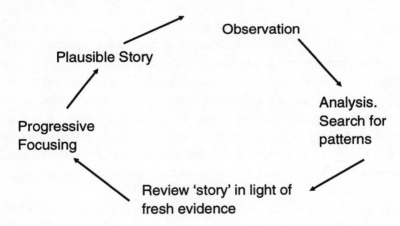

In the earliest stages of phase two, I took care to record in the daily diary anything that struck me as being of interest and potentially relevant. As the picture clarified and hypotheses developed about a pupil, I continued to try to be open to new ideas but observations became more focused. Throughout phase two, I paid attention to factors which might be important regardless of 'race' and background, but I paid specific attention to areas where 'race' and background issues might be relevant.

Teacher Interviews

A priority in designing the research was to obtain independent views about the classrooms and the twenty-five pupils, my own and the views of the teacher. Teachers' perspectives were sought through formal interviews in the middle of the Summer Term, using questions from a pre-prepared form.

During the interviews, I completed the forms for future quick reference. I used a general questionnaire to explore the teacher's perception of the classroom ethos and issues relating to 'race' and background, and a separate questionnaire on each child in the case studies. To ensure that my handwritten notes could be checked, the interviews were taped and later transcribed.

Ensuring that the teacher and I did not influence one another's views was difficult, since the teacher interviews had to take place while my observations were still in progress. As a compromise and to try to minimise the influence of a teacher's perspective on mine, I held the teacher interviews in the week before the summer half term holiday and delayed the analysis for several months. Only after the classroom observations were completed were my observations analysed and then, to minimise any risk of my perspective affecting the interpretation of the teacher's, there was a gap of two months while I worked on another project.

In analysing the interviews of each teacher, care was taken in interpreting what had been said and in considering alternative interpretations of the teacher's response to a question.

Pupil Achievement — Assessment in the National Curriculum

The Statutory Orders for the National Curriculum set out Attainment Targets (ATs) for each curriculum area. Teachers in the study were required by the Orders to give their own assessment of the level attained by each year two pupil in attainment targets in the three core curriculum subjects, English, mathematics and science. In addition, they had to use Standard Assessment Tasks (SATS) for an objective assessment of the level attained in seven targets, AT2, 3, 4 and 5 in English, AT3 and either AT12 or AT14 in mathematics, and AT6 or AT9 in science.

During the first term in school, I spent much time observing the SATS assessments and collecting, collating and analysing results for pupils of Caribbean heritage and also for each of the five classes as a whole. I hoped that these data would provide a third and objective measure of pupils' performance and that they could be used, firstly to compare performance of case study pupils with that of the rest of their class and, secondly, to compare the standard of achievement in the five classes. I also hoped that SATS results could be used to rank the performance of the twenty-five case study pupils.

Neither of these hopes was realised. The sample of classes was too small and results obtained by different classes were too diverse, given the small sample size, to compare ethnic minority success between classes. The problems of aggregation across ATs in one curriculum area, across curricula areas, and across classes, made it impossible to gain a measure of the relative achievement of each pupil. Different approaches to aggregation were tried, but the only firm conclusion was that four pupils were performing very well and two very poorly. For the remaining nineteen, no conclusions could be drawn.

The Research and its Analysis

The following chapters describe the research and its analysis. The gender of individual pupils and teachers is not indicated as this helps to preserve confidentiality. Instead all teachers are referred to as 'he', and all pupils as 'she'.

Chapter 4 examines pupils and their achievement. Chapter 5 looks at pupil and home variables in greater depth, and classroom factors are considered in chapter 6. The analysis is extended in chapter 7, with an in-depth examination of the effect of 'race' and background on pupils' classroom experiences and achievement.

Chapter 4

Achievement in Positive Classrooms

This chapter describes the research on pupil achievement. It draws on my author's classroom observations and interviews with teachers. Information from classroom observations were considered first then, after a gap of several months, the teacher interviews were reflected on. The interviews included twelve questions about each pupil (see end of chapter). The responses to the first questions provide a useful starting point for examining the influences on pupil achievement and so the chapter begins by discussing these.

What Teachers Thought

The teachers were interviewed about specific children. They were asked how they felt about the academic achievement of each child and to talk about three factors which they thought influenced the child to do well or poorly. The interview included a number of other questions, including some on 'race' and background issues, examined later in this chapter.

When the teachers' responses to these first questions were analysed, the following picture emerged. Of the twenty-five pupils in the case studies, teachers were reasonably satisfied with the academic attainment of eleven, but had reservations about fourteen, ranging from occasional disquiet to major and continuing concerns. Explaining their reasons, the teachers drew on their wide-ranging knowledge of individual pupils. They referred to such matters as performance in academic areas, sight vocabulary, reading, and written work. They compared what was achieved with their perception of the pupil's potential, using phrases like 'I'm not happy. She could do a lot better'. Occasionally, they commented on the pupil's progress or lack of it over the months. They focused on the behaviour of some pupils or their attendance, or both.

Pupils appeared to fall into distinct groups. Among the eleven pupils about whom teachers were reasonably happy three were perceived as very successful. They were seen as being above average in ability and a key factor in their success was perceived to be the supportiveness of parents who placed a high priority on education. This group is indicated in the following table as group 1 (see opposite).

A second group of five children with whose attainment teachers were happy were those for whom personal and social attributes were seen as helping to promote good behaviour, good work and success. Some of the phrases used about these pupils were: 'a sense of fairness', 'sensible', 'easily enthused and responds well', 'inquisitive', 'takes a pride in work and is interested', 'has lots of friends and is respected', 'a sense of humour'.

Of the two pupils in group 3, teachers thought their confidence contributed to their achievement. The eleventh pupil, shown as group 9, was found by the teacher to be 'a bit of a mystery'.

Among the remaining pupils, about whom teachers had reservations, there were five (group 4) for whom teachers felt lack of confidence was a major impediment to their achievement.

About the next three pupils, teachers were quite happy with their achievement but behaviour was a concern and occasional difficulties hindered or could hinder achievement (group 5). For another three, behaviour was perceived as a major and ongoing problem (group 6).

A twelfth child, placed in group 7, was performing moderately well but the teacher noted differences between spoken and written English and was slightly unhappy about it, asking tentatively whether the child might be a creole speaker and whether this contributed to the difference observed. This pupil had recently arrived from the Caribbean.

TEACHER PERCEPTIONS OF PUPILS		
Group	Teacher's Perspective	Number of Pupils
1	Very happy about attainment. Parents supportive. Value education. Pupil above average ability.	3
2	Happy about attainment. Conducive to achievement — Personal and Social Skills/Attitudes	5
3	Happy about attainment. Confidence of pupil helps	2
	Sub-Total	(10)
4	Lack of confidence reducing achievement/	5
5	Happy, but reservations. Occasional lapses, behaviour.	3
6	Behaviour a major concern.	3
7	Slight concern — mainly about written English (Pupil relatively recently arrived in UK)	1
8	Very concerned about pupil. Absences and lateness. Parent doesn't value education.	2
	Sub-Total	(14)
9	Quite happy but child a bit of a mystery	1
TOTAL NUMBER OF PUPILS		25

Finally, group 8 included two pupils about whom teachers were very concerned. They were seen as performing considerably below average due primarily to very poor attendance and frequent lateness. The situation of these pupils, in contrast with the children in group 1, was attributed to their parents not valuing education.

Teachers' responses to other questions about the pupils provided more detail about each child. When all questions had been analysed and these conclusions compared with my classroom observations, it emerged that the perceptions of the teachers and myself about whether or not pupil achievement was satisfactory were identical. The only exception were the pupils in group 2 who, as will be seen later, I thought to be performing well below their potential.

The view of pupils from the pupil questionnaires, and the picture obtained from my classroom observations, also coincide in highlighting the pupils' confidence and behaviour as key factors in achievement and in justifying the emphasis placed on them in the table on page 61. A useful framework for discussing pupil achievement is provided and the table will be referred to frequently in the rest of the chapter.

While the teachers and I came to similar conclusions about the relevance of confidence and behaviour, we differed in our perceptions of the degree of importance attributable to other variables underlying these factors. And there was a major difference between the two perspectives over the role played by 'race' and background.

I move now to accounts of individual children. This helps to depict the reality of the classroom and to draw out the variables which influence achievement. The description of the children is based on my development of case studies through the two terms, allowing a more rounded picture of each pupil than could be obtained in one interview with a teacher. For ease of exposition, discussion of 'race' and background influences will be delayed and examined at length in a separate chapter, even though these were considered throughout the development of case studies.

Classroom Observations of Pupils

During the two terms spent in schools, I observed a variety of tasks carried out by each pupil. I made notes of the pupil at work, of the quantity and quality of outcome, and of the pupil's discussions with other pupils. These data, complemented by informal conversations with the pupil, and opportunities to listen to pupils reading and to talk with them, were helpful in reflecting on each pupil's understanding and learning and hence in evaluating her/his level of achievement. They also helped in assessing whether the level and content of the task was appropriate for the pupil, and in gauging the pupil's potential ability and strengths.

Attention was paid to the pupil's response to each task, the way the pupil approached it, whether she/he appeared to enjoy working and be motivated, the degree of confidence, and general behaviour. Records were kept of situations, in or out of the classroom, which might help to evaluate a pupil's personal and social skills. Two semi-structured informal interviews with the pupils provided additional data and helped develop a picture of the whole pupil and of factors influencing her/his achievement.

For reasons of length, case studies are described for only eleven of the twenty-five pupils observed. The discussion follows the order of the groups in the table on page 61, describing all the pupils in the two extreme groups (i.e. 1 and 8), and including some pupils in groups 2, 4, and 6. These eleven pupils were chosen to give a representative picture of issues arising from the complete set of the twenty-five case studies.

Among the twenty-five pupils are four who regularly produced work of a high standard. Three of these are the group 1 pupils described now. From observation of these pupils at their tasks and discussions with them, it was clear that all were very able. One, a fluent and independent reader and an excellent mathematician, had wide interests, was good at analysis and extending ideas and was imaginative and creative. This was illustrated both by her unusual and unexpected comments in class and by responses made carrying out the Standard Assessment Task in Reading. This child had a strong awareness, articulated clearly to me in a semi-formal interview, about being 'good at stories and ideas' and having 'self confidence'.

Another pupil, also an excellent reader and imaginative, was very quick at picking up concepts and ideas. The third took an obvious pleasure in making connections and looking for and discovering patterns, and showed talent for imaginative and almost poetic use of language.

The reasons for the success of these three pupils were obvious. Apart from their ability, they were all children who appeared confident in their approach to the task and their relationships with others. They worked quickly and well, individually and in small group situations and their interest in their tasks was obvious. For two of the pupils, application to task appeared to come from an intrinsic motivation and personal satisfaction and one of them considered competition with others to be important. The third pupil appeared interested, but less so than the others, rather as if the child was working because it was expected by home and school.

All three pupils came from homes which valued education highly. This was evident from comments their parents made in school and from conversations with the children. Thus, one child talked about tapes bought and used at home and about Mum training to be a teacher because it was important. Another talked about Mum helping with reading at school and also about Mum's work in running playgroups. In the third case, the mother had been visiting a younger sibling in school daily and taking a keen interest and joy in what the child was learning. This valuing of education by parents undoubtedly contributed to the success of these pupils.

The approach of the three pupils to friends was interesting and different. For one, the tasks done and done extremely well, seemed less relevant than talking with special friends. All time in the playground was spent with these friends and the occasional contact made in the classroom was only when it was necessary to discuss unexpected events or for mutual support and security.

It appeared that the highest priority for this pupil was friendship and being respected as a natural leader in the friendship group. Academic successes contributed to status in the group and so to the pupil's motivation. The other two enjoyed their friendships, and relationships with others were good, but their position in the friendship group did not seem important for their fulfilment.

Classroom factors also contributed to the success of these pupils. They were all children who appeared to be especially valued by the teacher. This may have been partly the result of the pupils' success, but it helped to encourage and promote pupil confidence and success, and made it easier for teachers to give pastoral support and guidance when minor problems due to personality, interpersonal communications or outbursts occurred.

These three pupils then, seemed to have many influences working towards their success. The factors promoting success were their ability, confidence, task application and motivation, and classroom factors. For one, friendships and the status obtained as leader due to academic success also helped. Another child's wide interests were a contributory factor. It was noticeable that in spite of many commonalities, these children were very different from one another.

The three pupils described next, all in group 2, displayed certain common characteristics which could be expected to promote achievement. All appeared to be confident. Their behaviour was exemplary. They concentrated when working on the task set. Their relationship with other pupils was very good and they all appeared to be respected, trusted and sought out. Their relationship with their teachers was good. They had homes which valued education.

In spite of this, the impression I gained at an early stage was of underachievement. The first of the three, calm and articulate with friends and with the teacher, had an imagination evident in discussions and observation but which was not generally reflected in work done. The pupil worked consistently and solidly, but without using this imaginative talent, and without the enthusiasm which emerged in discussions with me.

The second pupil, very quiet and almost invisible, had surprised the teacher by performing unexpectedly well in reading in the SATS assessment. The child had enormous potential, as shown in an automatic analysing and questioning of stories when reading. She was also noticeably good at making connections, and had an unusual and apt sense of humour which emerged when discussing stories. Yet, in the classroom, tasks set were carried out well but slowly and without any strong interest or motivation. Not surprisingly, the quantity and quality of work appeared to be well below the child's potential.

The third pupil, more sensitive and shy in spite of being superficially confident, was very good at concentrating and getting on with the task. But progress was sometimes quite slow. Close observation suggested that she was not always as secure in the classroom as it seemed, did not in fact relate to the tasks, and the motivation to work arose primarily because the child accepted that it was expected by adults. When initially interviewed the children talked about what they liked doing, what they were good at, and what made them happy. The response of this child was unique: 'School makes me happy. It's a good class. Fun. I like learning.' This confident and positive verbal statement contrasted with the pupil's uncertain and somewhat unhappy demeanour when making it.

The work produced by this pupil was less good than might have been expected given her usually confident exterior. The poor performance could be attributed to reservations and worries about maths and about presenting things well, but this did not appear to explain the tentative response to classroom activities. It seemed to me that the reason might lie in an insecurity linked to this rather sensitive pupil's awareness of other people's perceptions of differences associated with being black.

For these three pupils, all confident, with supportive homes valuing education, well-behaved and with good concentration and social skills, the main barrier to full achievement appeared to be lack of drive in application to tasks. The reasons underlying this differed for, like the group 1 children, pupils in this group were quite different from one another.

Only two of the five group 4 pupils are discussed here. The work produced by the first was not only below the standard the pupil was capable of, but was incomplete. This pupil appeared capable of performing at the same standard as pupils in group 1, and was well above average in reading, as shown by the SATS. Although 'bright' and with a 'supportive Mum', her performance was generally poor, she lacked motivation and concentration, and her on-task behaviour was far from ideal.

It seemed to me that the key to poor performance and factors contributing to it lay in the child's relationships with other children. There were frequent lapses in her behaviour in relation to other children. She could be quite nasty and sometimes spiteful and part of her difficulties appeared to arise from poor interpersonal relationships, and a resentment and unhappiness linked to an inability to make friends. This in turn contributed to lack of confidence at school. When talking about home, she was less resentful and more confident.

The second pupil in group 4 described here, although also lacking confidence, was very different. This child appeared to me to be motivated and interested in work, especially in science, and concentrated well on the tasks set. The pupil had a strong personality and was quite an extrovert, very articulate and with a talent for dramatic expressiveness.

Lack of confidence, the main cause of unsatisfactory work, seemed at times to be associated with anxiety about doing maths. More frequently, it seemed more associated with the awkwardness of a pupil with a strong personality who was still developing and learning about interpersonal relations. The child seemed to have potential leadership skills and to be a good organiser, but in spite of being very articulate in talking about abstract things, was not always able to communicate in an acceptable way and on occasion seemed unaware of how others were responding. Sometimes, problems were handled by mild confrontation or 'bloody mindedness'. Behaviour was not a major problem, but it could have been.

Thus, for the two children described, interpersonal skills were an important barrier to full achievement. No children in group 5 are described here (but one of these, a pupil performing very well academically, is described in the section at the end of the chapter on high achievers), and the description continues with a pupil in group 6.

The behaviour of this child was a major problem. Poor behaviour was so frequent and so extreme that it prevented success in carrying out tasks and reduced achievement significantly. Manifestations of poor behaviour included not settling down to the task set, being very restless, being verbally nasty and aggressive to other pupils and quarrelling with them. Behaviour was not always poor, and there were occasions, sometimes weeks, when the pupil worked well and to good effect, and it was difficult to explain what caused phases of deterioration in behaviour.

According to the teacher, fluctuations were linked to happenings at home. This differed from my perception. From looking at pictures with this pupil and talking with her about some of her work, it seemed to me that there might be other, underlying factors: the pupil was very confident but at the same time gave me an impression of confusion. Closer and more careful observation, of the things she said and the way she said them, suggested that her home was very structured, with clear and stated boundaries for behaviour. School and home were very different in these respects and the pupil found it difficult to reconcile these differences. The teacher was not aware of this or that there was more explicit guidance at home and nore control.

An additional difficulty was that the child seemed to be trying to resolve conflicting and personal feelings of great importance to her self-image: a strong feeling that people of African descent are better than others and the possibility that this might be untrue.

In short, it seemed likely to me that pressures in school for this pupil may have emanated from the teacher's lack of knowledge of aspects of Caribbean sub-culture, and from the pupil's need to articulate and discuss her feelings about roots.

The two children in group 8 described next also had major problems. For them, there were no successes and their work was frequently inadequate. A major cause was their poor attendance, which was evident throughout my field work.

One child was absent for long periods at a time, once when her mother was away from home. Another time the child was ill and failed to return to school when recovered. The register showed that this child had missed about one-third of the term.

My informal interviews with a teacher who worked with the child and knew her and her family well, suggested that poor attendance and lateness were due to her mother's lack of interest in education. Nevertheless, according to this teacher, the child was adored and much loved at home.

This pupil's work was frequently unfinished and significantly below average in both quantity and quality. Her extremely poor behaviour contributed to this. She was very nervy, disrupted others, was unable to settle and concentrate, and liable to provoke stormy and confrontational exchanges with other children.

While some of this behaviour was due to the difficulties arising from frequent absences, some appeared to be due to the pupil's own tendency to place a low value on education relative to the more exciting and important happenings at home. On some occasions, from remarks she suddenly made, it appeared that the inability to settle was partly linked with a preoccupation with home and the fact that this pupil had 'lots to occupy ... my mind after school'.

Nevertheless, the pupil was very bright, quick at concepts and numbers, and showed a self-confidence, an independence and a strong valuing of self which made it possible for her to try to rise to the challenges and demands arising from being in a very difficult situation at school.

The other child was frequently late or absent, arriving halfway through the morning or even after lunch. Occasionally the mother took the child shopping during school hours, as I discovered in informal conversation. A support teacher who knew the child and the family said that the mother had had unhappy school experiences and consequently a negative attitude to education and gave it low priority.

Her child seemed potentially able, with her own ideas, a good memory and analytical potential, and a desire to do well. But in class she appeared to be just stolidly surviving, using a coping strategy of avoiding problems with the teacher and keeping a low profile generally. So when she arrived late one morning, dressed up for a special school occasion but at playtime and too late to take part in it, she sat calmly inside on her own. When I approached her, she tried to avoid contact with me, talking in a silly and babyish way. I persevered, and suddenly she switched into a normal and chatty mode, talking interestingly about school and her home, including the family's many black relations and friends.

That the child was quite bright was clear. Once, on her return to school after a period of absence, she was included in a small group of pupils being assessed in science. She was initially silent in the group discussion, then made some very relevant comments in spite of being away for so long. Unfortunately, she spoke so quietly that the teacher did not hear. And as the session continued and the teacher tried to solicit the answers he expected, the child retreated more and more and performed increasingly badly.

This pupil had no problems in settling down to work and, indeed, seemed to have a good attitude to working. Nevertheless, her work was consistently of a poor standard, caused partly, it seemed, by her own low valuing of herself.

So, for both these pupils, while an important barrier to achievement was poor attendance, there were other factors, different for the two, which affected outcomes and potential outcomes. For one, poor concentration was a key. A somewhat nervous disposition combined with a lack of valuing of school, a lack of motivation and a preoccupation with other priorities inhibited achievement. The second child's low value of herself and her low profile strategy for handling difficult situations prevented her achievement.

Both children's teachers felt frustrated. Their frustration was very obvious to me and to their classes, and also to the pupils concerned. Interestingly, their feelings were manifested very differently. One teacher frequently expressed intense anger with the parent who could harm a child's future in such a way and exasperation with the child and her behaviour. The irritation directed towards the child was combined with consistent exhortations to behave and do well. There were frequently explosions of 'I don't know what to do with this child', and yet, an almost personal satisfaction 'you see, you can do it,' when the child had some success. Throughout the period of observation, the teacher's high expectations of this pupil and the work she could produce was evident.

The other teacher's frustration appeared to lead to a condemnation of the family and occasional wonderment and virtual contempt for them. This teacher consistently expressed anger at the child and what looked not unlike distaste and dislike for the family and child. And, perhaps because of his frustrations over his own inability to cure the basic problem of lateness and non-attendance, he focused on this rather than on other causes of this child's underachievement.

Pupil Achievement

The descriptions of individual pupils reveal the difficulties which some young children can face at school and which can be quite severe. Children who are often late or absent, like the children in group 8, can find school an unhappy or unfulfilling experience. In other cases, schooling can be difficult as children, still developing, try to handle the variety of challenges they face and the differences between home and school. Some find solutions. Some cope but still fail to give of their best. Some flounder and are bewildered and confused by the differences between home and school and ongoing stresses as they try to develop the ability to handle difficult situations.

Confidence and behaviour appear to be key variables affecting achievement. For the highest and the lowest achievers amongst these children, ability and the value attached by the home to education also seem important. Confidence on the part of a pupil and/or very high ability can contribute to progress, while lack of confidence, poor behaviour and a home which places a low priority on education hinders progress.

One also needs to consider the effect of the way children approach tasks i.e. their on-task application. Motivation, the pupil's own agenda and priorities, her security and confidence, and the extent to which she relates to the task set are all contributory influences. School-home differences may play a part when school does not reflect the home and the child does not relate to what is being taught, or when differences cause confusion for the child.

Children's personal and social skills are also important. These determine the nature of relationships with other children, so can influence their behaviour or confidence. They also determine the child's ability to handle difficult situations and the strategies used to cope with them.

It is clear that a simplistic approach, based on a mathematical model where the variables identified influence outcomes in a clearly defined way, might not be valid. Relevant variables can be interrelated — the extent depends on the pupil concerned. Pupils' differing personalities, their personal/social attributes and skills contribute to difficulties in predicting the processes through which achievement is affected, the variables which are relevant and the size of the effect of these on outcomes.

Teachers' Perspectives on 'Race' and Cultural Background

Before going on to look at particular groups of pupils, a brief description of the conclusions concerning teachers' perceptions of the effects of 'race' and background will be helpful.

Teachers did not generally bring the child's 'race' and cultural background into answering questions about achievement. Only in two cases did this occur, once about a pupil lacking confidence, and once with a pupil who had recently arrived from the Caribbean.

Because I had foreseen that 'race' and background issues might be omitted, I asked questions to ensure that these were discussed. One question which proved useful, inquired whether the teacher thought that the fact that the pupil being discussed was black and had a Caribbean background had any relevance to the pupil's progress. Teachers found this question very difficult to respond to, but they took their time and reflected and eventually gave an answer. They answered confidently in some cases and very tentatively in others.

Teachers' responses to these specific questions suggested that factors arising from pupils' 'race' and background were not typically seen as affecting achievement. For the handful of children whose achievement was said to be suffering, the teachers were very uncertain about whether what they were saying was justified. The fact that one child, recently arrived from the Caribbean, might speak creole, was discussed as a possible factor. For other pupils, it was the indirect effects of racism that teachers thought might be potentially relevant. The teacher asked whether these pupils might suffer from stresses and pressures on their homes, arising from the additional disadvantages experienced by black families.

The confidence of another two pupils was thought by teachers to suffer, both of them children with one white parent. One child's behaviour was said to have been very unsettled and the teacher asked, very tentatively whether the child might have an inner feeling of not belonging. About the second child, the teacher asked whether the lack of initiative and apparent inferiority complex was due to being of mixed race in a class where most of the pupils of Caribbean background were, to quote a pupil in another class, 'fully black'.

Teachers also thought that it was true of a few children that they had experienced negative effects in the past. One child had come from Africa and might, a teacher said, have experienced language problems. Stereotyping by teachers in previous years, or racial harassment by pupils in previous schools, were mentioned about other children.

For a few pupils, 'race' and background were thought to play a positive role. A teacher noted how aware and positive one pupil was about being black and the child's interest in her links with Jamaica. He mentioned her pride and confidence in her roots, and the benefits from having a positive family structure and being a secure member of an extended family.

In short, 'race' and background appeared to have a low profile in teachers' considerations of barriers to current achievement and were occasionally thought to have a positive effect. This contrasted noticeably with my perceptions, as explored in chapter 7.

High Achievers

Four pupils among the twenty-five in the case studies could be described as high achievers: the three in group 1 and one pupil in group 5 whose work was of a very high standard but about whom the teacher was not entirely happy. This child had not always produced work of this quality, and had had behavioural problems that were quite serious at the beginning of the school year but occurred only occasionally in the middle of the summer term when the teacher interviews took place. It is interesting to look at these pupils to see whether there are any clues as to why some children of Caribbean background succeed while others do not.

What appeared to me to distinguish these pupils from others was that several factors promoting achievement were all operating and the key to their excellent performance was a cycle of success. This pattern was self-generating, promoting confidence in carrying out tasks, motivation and interest on the part of the child and special valuing on the part of the teacher. For two of the four pupils, it appeared that this had not always been the case and and it is worth exploring whether their history gives us any clearer answers other than the rather trite one, that 'success breeds success'.

One of the two, a pupil in group 1, had had prolonged periods of very poor behaviour in the first phase of my time in classrooms i.e. when my focus was on classrooms rather than on individual pupils. In the words of the teacher at a later interview, the child had 'not been getting down to work, arguing, fighting, constantly answering back, stealing'. Not surprisingly, during this period, her performance had not been good. Consistent efforts were made by the teacher and the child's mother to keep in touch about her misbehaviour and any improvements. This, combined with a timely and fortunate breakthrough in reading, appears to have been instrumental in helping her to move on. Support from all concerned concentrated on highlighting and praising any progress she made.

This pupil appeared to be disadvantaged by family hardships and to suffer from the economic and other pressures on the family. Generally she read very well, quickly and fluently, but when pressures were particularly acute, she would appear preoccupied and dazed and have moments of forgetfulness, at times peering at the book as if not seeing it.

Academic success, once started, was consistent despite problems at home. The ability to continue to cope academically and behave well at school appeared to be possible because of the child's determination and the closeness, warmth and mutual support between mother and child and the mother's very strong valuing of education. The child wanted to do well and was interested in tasks set so tried to behave appropriately and was, moreover, influenced by a desire to please Mum.

For the pupil in group 5, there had been steady improvement rather than a sudden breakthrough. Said by the teacher to need attention because of being in the middle of a large family, this child had a tendency initially to 'be stubborn, to talk non-stop to herself, and do things which drew attention to herself'. She would do unacceptable things such as remaining standing defiantly after the class sat down on the carpet. The teacher found that the best strategy was to praise her regularly. Instead of provoking confrontation and greater behavioural problems, the teacher acknowledged the child's accomplishments, praising her when she did something without being asked or performed academic tasks well, finding that private praise was as effective as public.

These two children, then, were completely different, and the role of their parents in improvement was important in one case and not the other. However, a common element in both stories was the teacher's acknowledgement of the pupil's progress, which had a dual and beneficial effect. It made the pupils aware of their steps towards success, and it highlighted the fact that they were valued and that their academic improvement was of importance to their teacher. Both aspects contributed to breaking the pattern of underachievement and/or poor behaviour and helped to move these pupils onto a self-generating cycle of success.

The other two pupils described as high achievers, both in group 1, and the last child in group 5 will be discussed further in chapter 7 in which the role of 'race' and background is explored. (See Pupil Nine and Ten (page 128) and Pupil One (page 119)). We shall see that for the last pupil these may have been and possibly still were preventing full achievement.

Very Low Achievers

This chapter would not be complete without a discussion of what teachers were doing to try to promote achievement by very low achievers. We now look briefly at the group 6 pupil whose behaviour was of major concern (see page 67), and the two pupils in group 8.

One strategy used with the poorly-behaved pupil in group 6, was to liaise very closely with her parents, keeping in touch two or three times a week about her behaviour. This was easy because her parents were themselves concerned about what was happening at school, valued education and were keen to support the teacher. The teacher tried also to make it possible for the child to behave well by providing space for her to work separately and without distraction. These strategies were effective in stopping the most extreme behaviour, although the child's behaviour tended to fluctuate.

I wondered whether the lack of sustained improvement was due to the deeper underlying problems, already discussed on page 67, which were not being tackled by the teacher or parents.

Contact with the parents of one of the children in group 8, a very disruptive child, was eventually made and she sometimes went home for lunch, so creating a little space and peace for the child and the class. She was also given some extra individual support. These strategies, the fact that this child was well able to rise to challenges, and the continuing high expectations of the teacher may all have contributed to the small though noticeable improvement in her behaviour and work.

Contact with the parent of the second child in group 8 — the low-profile child — was eventually made and the child was paired with another for support when she arrived at school late. That significant improvement was not made appeared to me to be due to a lack of valuing of herself on the part of the child, and her coping strategy of adopting a very low profile.

Teacher interviews showed that they saw providing reassurance as important for children generally. This approach was especially appropriate for these three children in view of the potential difficulties they faced in the classroom. But a strategy of providing reassurance was not evident during observations nor mentioned in interviews about these three pupils, perhaps because of the teachers' pre-occupation with what were seen as immediate and extreme problems of coping with children disrupting a whole class by suddenly arriving after a long absence, or by exhibiting very poor and disruptive behaviour. This partly explains the lack of acceptable and sustained improvement for two of the three pupils, but the teachers' ignoring of 'race' and background issues may also have played a part.

For the group 6 pupil, there were difficulties due to the differences between home and school due to arising from 'Caribbean' aspects of home, and due to the child's perceptions of being black and different. The group 8 low-profile child's low values of self appeared to be exacerbated by her awareness that being black is perceived by some as being from an inferior community. These and other issues relating to 'race' and background are considered at length in chapter 7.

Summing Up

The teacher interviews about each of the twenty-five pupils suggest that pupils could be placed into specific categories according to the teachers' perceptions of the role played by their confidence and behaviour. Some pupils were doing extremely well and appeared to have a number of advantageous influences: ability, confidence and motivation, parental support and valuing of education. For pupils at the other extreme, the key factor was their parents' lack of valuing education, manifested in pupil absences and lateness.

'Race' and children's cultural backgrounds were not generally considered by teachers when evaluating achievement. My observations suggest that these may be important.

In other respects, there was considerable overlap between the teachers' view of individual children and mine. The main differences arose about a small number of pupils with whose progress teachers were satisfied while I was not and, for some other children, determining which were the most important influences on their achievement.

The key variables identified in this chapter are confidence, motivation and application to task, behaviour, children's own agendas and priorities, and their personal and social skills. In the case of high achievers, several factors promoting achievement appeared to be contributing to good performance and they seemed to be on a cycle of self-generating success. For two children, moving to this stage seemed to have depended on praise from the teacher, the child's own awareness of steps towards success and the teacher's recognition and valuing of their progress. The reasons for the poor achievement of the very low achievers, appeared to differ from child to child.

Finally, although the case studies suggested that there are key variables which can be identified for a theory of achievement, they also showed that it is impossible to generalise or to predict what the situation will be for a specific pupil of Caribbean heritage. Each child is an individual, the relevant variables differ, and the processes through which their achievement is influenced by key variables are very diverse.

Appendix to Chapter 4

Pupil Questionnaire

1. How long has X been in your class?

2. How do you feel about X's academic attainment, happy or concerned?

3. Could you explain why?

4. Do you know X's parents from parents' evenings?
   What do you know about them and the rest of the family?

5. Can you tell me three influences which you think help X to do well.., which prevent it?

6. What was X like when he/she first came into your class?

7. Who are X's friends in the class?

8. Comparing different curricular areas, do you think X has any noticeable specific strengths or specific weaknesses?

   (Followed by:) Could you tell me what you did to help X to develop further?

9. Looking at the achievement of X, do you think that the fact that she/he is black and has a Caribbean background has/has had any relevance to her/his progress?

10. Do you think that X thinks of his/herself as black?

11. How does X feel about his/herself as a (black) British child, with Caribbean roots?

12. Has X ever been called names or teased because of being black?

Chapter 5

Pupil and Home Variables

While chapter 4 examined pupil achievement, it did not look in any depth at specific pupil and home variables or investigate teachers' perceptions of the nature of such variables. It seems important to clarify the latter in view of the emphasis placed in the past on deficit theories which problematised the home and the child of Caribbean heritage. This chapter, a short one, seeks to do this.

Patterns in Teachers' Perceptions

This section is based on the two questions on achievement in the pupil questionnaires i.e. those concerning the teacher's satisfaction or otherwise with a child's attainment, and the influences on the achievement. When talking about the twenty-five case study pupils, teachers mentioned home and pupil variables in equal measure, making twenty-seven mentions in each case, sometimes referring to a pupil more than once. As the table

No. of Pupils Involved	Total	Negative Effect Only	Other
Home Variables	20	8	12
Pupil Variables	23	13	10

shows, home variables were brought up for twenty pupils and pupil variables for twenty-three.

For eight pupils affected by home variables and thirteen by pupil variables their effect was thought to reduce achievement. But on other occasions, these variables were brought up as fostering the pupil's achievement or having both beneficial and harmful effects. This applied to twelve pupils for whom home variables were mentioned and ten for whom pupil variables came up.

A closer look at these variables provides useful insight into the teachers' perceptions about which variables hinder achievement and which help to foster it. The table below shows the results of separating parental support variables from other home-related variables, and pupil behaviour from other pupil-related variables:

No. of Pupils Involved	Total	Effect Solely Negative	Effect Solely Positive	Both Effects
Parental support	13	2	11	0
Other	14	11	3	0
All Home Variables	(20)			
Pupil behaviour	9	8	1	0
Relating to pupil	18	8	8	2
All Pupil Variables	(23)			

The breakdown of home variables suggests that parents were perceived as supportive, since this was true of all but two of thirteen instances when parental support was mentioned. In contrast, other variables connected with the pupils' homes were frequently thought to hinder achievement. The table clearly shows that when referring to pupil variables, the teachers were thinking predominantly of behaviour which hindered achievement, whereas this was less true for other pupil variables.

As the interviews progressed, teachers talked about what pupils had been like when they first came into the class, about their curricular strengths and weaknesses, their friendships and families. This provided additional examples of pupil and home variables. The rest of this chapter draws on these data as well as those gathered from the initial two questions in the interview. As will be seen, the pattern observed from the initial questions was duplicated when all the responses were analysed.

What The Home Contributes

Chapter 2 discussed the first deficit theory of achievement, that which focused on families and homes, and referred to variables such as the academic and emotional/physical support of the child, the structure of the family, discipline at home, and disadvantages arising from 'race' and socio-economic background. In the 1950s and 60s these had largely been seen as causing 'underachievement', as the diagram on page 40 illustrates.

The analysis of the teacher questionnaires shows that thirty years on, there are teachers who do not adhere to this deficit view and who value parents and the role they play in education. Parents of sixteen of the twenty-five case study pupils were thought to be interested in their child's academic development and supportive to school. Parental contacts were referred to briefly about another three and these appeared to be satisfactory, and for three no reference was made to parental support. Only for three pupils were concerns expressed about the support provided.

That parents were interested in education was manifested at different levels. Among the sixteen sets of supportive parents were some who actively promoted work at home. Where teachers had Shared Reading Schemes and pupils took reading books home, parents encouraged their children to read them. Also, although pupils were not given specific homework, some parents encouraged reading or writing at home. There were sometimes books around the house, including stories or information, or books with mathematical puzzles. One parent had bought a song tape to help her child learn tables.

The interest of parents was also evident in their partnership with teachers about children's academic progress and their contacts with teachers about it. A few of the sixteen parents perceived as supportive, made contact only through the school's annual or biannual parents' evenings, but many did so much more frequently. Several talked with teachers at least once a fortnight, usually when collecting or bringing children to school, and parents would come more often if concerned about their child's progress. To quote one teacher speaking about a pupil's parents: 'They came in after school, evenings... anytime. They used to come in to help choose reading. They haven't been in for a while so I expect they are pleased with her progress.'

Certain parents seemed to take a specific interest in schooling. Five put much time and effort into helping in their children's schools. Three went into school weekly to hear pupils read. A fourth supported a major multicultural project, visiting the class several times during this project, taking in resources, and giving a talk to the whole class. Two of the four were school governors and put additional time into the many tasks that governors perform. A fifth parent, also a governor, devoted time to the routine duties of governors and frequently attended assemblies and other school activities.

Other parents who did not participate as actively as these five nevertheless had a strong personal interest in education. One parent was studying to become a teacher and another organised and ran playgroups for pre-school children. Thus, seven of the sixteen supportive parents were actively involved in education and there were only three pupils for whom teachers explicitly referred to problems associated with a lack of parental support. Two were the group 8 pupils (page 61). Their parents had not made informal contact with the teacher or attended parents' evenings until the teacher/headteacher insisted that they visit the school. About the third pupil, the teacher told me: 'I have never seen the parents. They don't come in, even to parents' evenings. Brothers bring the child to school.' The child was 'a bit of a mystery' and teacher-parent contact might have provided some insight to help her progress.

The effect of other home variables was perceived very differently to parental support. Home variables were seen as having a beneficial effect on the achievement of three of the pupils. Skills and values in these three families were perceived as crucial determinants of the pupils' own personal skills and as fostering their achievement. But the benefits for these pupils (all in group 2) were not typical. In many more cases, twelve in all, teachers referred to variables connected with homes which hindered achievement.

The most common of the negative home variables related to upbringing and was mentioned for five of the twenty-five pupils. For one pupil with young parents, it was the complete lack of structure at home which the teacher thought particularly relevant. A second pupil was described as the youngest in the family, loved to the point of being spoiled and said not to have to take any responsibility for what she did. A third was much valued but 'never criticised at home'. The last two were thought to suffer because of undue parental anxieties and pressures about their progress. Parents restricted what the children did at home lest friends might distract them from work. In no case did teacher concerns appear to centre on, or be associated with, a perception that the upbringing in families of Caribbean backgrounds was problematic.

Occasionally, it was not upbringing but lifestyles or family structure that was mentioned, for example, that one pupil 'needed a lot of praise' because of being 'in the middle of a large family'. Another had a working parent said to spend too little time with the child.

Events at home were thought to be important for three of the twenty-five pupils. One was said to be insecure because her parents were about to separate. Two of the children were moody, and this seemed to be related to things at home: in one case, the father, who was much respected by the teacher, had to go abroad for reasons connected with work.

Finally, the pupil recently arrived from the Caribbean was perceived as having difficulties. The teacher asked whether problems with written English arose because she spoke creole. The pupil had in fact had greater difficulties the previous year, finding the weather uncomfortably cold and needing considerable support for several months in settling in and making friends. The teacher involved was quite concerned and sympathetic.

On balance, it was clear that teachers were not advocating or subscribing to a deficit theory about families and homes. Two-thirds of the parents were seen as supportive and valuing education, some very actively so. In several of the cases where variables associated with home were thought to hinder achievement, parents were seen as interested in their children's education. In the words of a teacher speaking about a particular parent, they were 'keen to have things happen for their child, and acted supportively in many ways'.

Parents were generally perceived as loving and caring. Where problems linked to homes did exist, they appeared to have a wide range of causes, and could have been relevant for children of any background, so teachers did not assume that families were problematic because of their Caribbean backgrounds. Pupils and parents seemed to be generally valued and liked by all five of the teachers.

Pupil Variables

As discussed in chapter 2, the attributing of lesser achievement by pupils of Caribbean heritage to an inherently low IQ was common when a theory of pupil deficit prevailed. The theory's legacy has been the stereotyping of such pupils as less intelligent and low teachers' expectations of them.

This did not appear to be the case for the five teachers in the study. Their attitudes to ability emerged from their responses to questions about pupils' curricular strengths and weaknesses and from other comments that they made in the interview about pupils' abilities. Only for three pupils were comments made which suggested that they were perceived as slower and less able to pick up concepts. Indeed, of the twenty one pupils for whom their teachers' perceptions of their ability emerged, seven were perceived as of above average ability.

Other pupil variables mentioned were almost exclusively restricted to the pupils' behaviour, confidence, personal skills and attributes and their motivation/attitude to school. The table summarises the effects described:

No. of Pupils Involved	Total	Effect Solely Negative	Effect Solely Positive	Both Effects
Ability	21	3	18	
Behaviour	19	15	2	2
Confidence	17	10	7	
Personal/ Social Attributes	17	8	4	5
Motivation/ Attitude	15	5	10	

Behaviour was brought up on twenty-one occasions and in almost all cases the description was of poor behaviour. Nineteen pupils were mentioned and the behaviour of fifteen seen as wholly detrimental to their achievement. However, as in the case of variables connected with the home, teachers did not reveal a deficit/problem approach to this group of pupils. Children were generally liked and respected and the behaviour described did not arise from stereotyping those of Caribbean heritage as having deviant behaviour, but from an assumption that normal children of any background need support and guidance in the development of appropriate behaviour.

Many types of behaviour were mentioned. Teachers referred frequently to the children's task orientation, for example, their 'poor concentration', 'slowness in working' and 'lack of perseverance'. Behaviour in relation to other pupils also arose: 'problems in forming relationships', 'an inability to take criticism or handle differences in opinion', and one child who 'can be a bully especially with weaker children'. Teachers discussed the reactions of children to them, and described incidents of children being 'deliberately contrary' or 'truculent' and 'rude'. Manifestations of behaviour associated with emotional needs came up. Teachers talked about children 'requiring an unusual amount of reassurance', 'seeking attention' or being 'very unsettled or distraught on arrival at school'.

References to pupils' confidence did not reflect a deficit approach to this group of children. Confidence was identified as a significant factor for seventeen pupils. For only ten of the twenty-five pupils was lack of confidence said to be or to have been a problem, and in most cases it was seen as something that could affect a child of any background.

In a few cases, lack of confidence was associated with what were regarded as psychological barriers, in particular academic areas, especially maths, but it was more frequently said about attitudes to work generally. Difficulties in working independently were mentioned less often and so were pupils' interactions with other pupils. One pupil's reluctance to take a high profile was mentioned and her lack of confidence in presenting ideas to the class or participating in small group discussions was seen as hindering progress. The strategies that teachers described to develop confidence in pupils of Caribbean heritage were similar to strategies recommended for white pupils.

Similarly, other personal/social attributes and skills were sometimes seen as assets but more often thought to hinder achievement. For eight of the seventeen pupils for whom variables of this type were mentioned, the effects were purely negative but for another five effects were both negative and positive.

Some of these variables influenced the children's interactions with others. This was so for the child described as 'spiteful', and for 'a child that the others are scared of' and true, too, for 'a child respected by others' who was further described as having 'good communication skills and an ability to recognise, listen, and consider other pupils' perspectives'.

The children's behaviour or the way they handled situations was also influenced by this set of variables. Certain children were described as 'unaware of boundaries', 'unaware of the consequences of their behaviour', or 'unable to control sudden outbursts'. One very difficult child was described as 'very volatile and doesn't take any responsibility for herself'. There were also positive comments like 'she takes responsibility for herself'.

The way pupils approached work was seen as relevant: whether pupils took responsibility for their learning, whether they were able to work independently and with others. One child was said to be 'a perfectionist, very slow and can't be hurried up..she is thrown by anything going out of order'.

The issue of motivation was thought relevant for fifteen pupils. It was seen as helping to promote the achievement of ten of the fifteen, who were said to apply themselves well and to have a good attitude to school. For the remaining five, motivation was thought to be poor and seen as a potential problem.

It is clear from these descriptions that teachers in the study were aware of pupil-related negative influences on achievement. This does not mean that they supported a deficit theory of achievement. IQ levels did not figure in their responses and several children were perceived as of above average ability. Teachers commented on the behaviour of several children, but their comments were not restricted to disruptive behaviour. None of the five teachers appeared to stereotype the case study children.

Low self-esteem was not raised as an issue. Confidence was perceived as an important variable, but teachers saw some children as confident. When they thought that a certain child of Caribbean heritage lacked confidence, teachers responded with a range of appropriate strategies to foster it, and did not immediately assume that self-esteem was low because of their backgrounds.

Conclusions

This study used an extremely small sample of teachers in Britain, chosen from 'positive' schools i.e. schools thought to be interested in meeting the needs of pupils of Caribbean heritage. The research suggests that this small group of selected teachers did not hold a deficit view of pupils of Caribbean heritage and their families.

There were home and pupil related variables which hindered achievement, but there were also positive influences. Children and their parents were liked and valued. It also emerges that parents in the study were supportive, keen to encourage the academic development of their children, and worked towards this at different levels, some giving up considerable time to support the work of the school.

Chapter 6

Teachers and Classrooms

Chapter 6 continues the description and analysis of the 1992 research and explores the second and third of the four questions set out in chapter 3 (on page 53). Using the research located in five 'positive' classrooms, it describes and assesses models in these classrooms for promoting achievement, and examines the 'messages' given to pupils about their 'race' and background. It goes on to identify classroom factors which influence the achievement of pupils of Caribbean heritage.

As discussed in the section on the field research in chapter 3, classroom observations for this phase of the research were guided by two general principles. One was getting to know the classroom. The second was identifying any and every occasion on which 'race' might be impinging on teacher activities or children's experiences. Observations were initially open-ended and unstructured and became more focused in the second part of this phase of the field work.

The chapter draws on these observations and also on the General Questionnaire completed during the teacher interviews in the middle of the summer term (see page 116). Great care was taken in interpreting what teachers said, and in trying to ensure that my observations were not influenced by teachers' perspectives and that the analysis of the teachers' perceptions in no way reflected my views.

The Five Classrooms — Teachers' Perceptions

While the main objective was to determine each teacher's perception of her/his model for promoting achievement, it was hoped that light would be thrown on areas generally thought to have implications for the academic progress of pupils of Caribbean heritage. Was multicultural work prioritised by teachers and, if so, why? What were the expectations and standards in these classrooms? Were they any different for black pupils? Were the teachers strongly aware of racism and, if so, did their philosophy of teaching reflect this? How were incidents of racial harassment perceived? How were different groups of pupils perceived and related to?

The ten questions used in the General Questionnaire are given at the end of this chapter. They were phrased and organised to enable teachers to talk about what they thought important and to determine their achievement-fostering model but they were designed to ensure also that certain key issues were discussed.

The table on the next page summarises responses to the first section of the questionnaire. Philosophies about teaching differed and this influenced the teachers' strategies for promoting the achievement of pupils of Caribbean heritage.

The first teacher regarded planning and organisation to meet individual needs as a crucial element of the classroom for all children. He prioritised creating an environment in which pupils valued and respected other pupils' views, and in which learning was fun. When he was asked how the children knew his standards of behaviour, he was clear about the significance of each pupil's view. He referred to discussions with the whole class about standards of behaviour. He showed the 'ground rules for the class which the children drew up. I didn't impose them'. The list started with the need to listen to one another and reinforced its priority:

LISTEN TO ONE ANOTHER
WE TAKE TURNS
TAKE CARE OF ONE ANOTHER
BE KIND ALWAYS
TAKE CARE OF OUR EQUIPMENT
ALWAYS TIDY UP

TEACHER PERCEPTIONS — HOW TO PROMOTE ACHIEVEMENT

Teacher	Do pupils underachieve (Q1)	Promoting achievement pupils, Caribbean heritage (Q3)	Important — all pupils (Q4)
A	Yes	Focus — individual pupil need. Appropriate work. Teacher awareness of how pupil may be affected.	Plan, organise, for individual academic need. Learning is fun. Environment where pupils respect others' views and needs.
B	Yes	Bring in backgrounds — to inspire pupils, make them feel valued.	Pupils to know they are valued by teacher, and a lot is expected. Environment needs to be exciting, full of stimuli.
C	No	Use multicultural resources, books materials. See parents as a resource.	Build on experiences, backgrounds. See child as individual, in and out of school. Teacher to stay as calm as possible.
D	Yes	Bring in background where opportunity arises and is appropriate. Monitor and ensure equal opportunities across the curriculum.	Plan, organise. Ensure pupils have sense of direction. Tasks to be interesting.
E	No	Treat the same as any child. Help when need help. Tick off as would any other child.	Promote pupil personal development through talk. Empathy for concerns. (Clear standards.)

This teacher thought that the pupils of Caribbean heritage were under-achieving and that the remedy depended on planning and setting work designed to 'boost identified weaknesses' and to 'extend strengths'. He also saw pastoral care as relevant and stressed that although it was important not to see problems where they did not exist, and not to intrude clumsily or unnecessarily into private areas, teachers needed to be sensitive to the possibility that children's experiences might be affected negatively by being black, and their behaviour and confidence suffer.

The second and fourth teachers, B and D, both stressed the need to create an interesting and inspiring environment. One said that 'the environment needs to be stimulating, full of stimuli' and the other talked about how to make tasks interesting. Accordingly, both teachers saw a need to bring in the children's Caribbean backgrounds.

Like the first teacher, Teacher D's class had talked about desirable standards of behaviour and the teacher had drawn up a short-list for everyone to remember:

TREAT OTHERS AS YOU WOULD LIKE TO BE TREATED

TREAT EVERYTHING WITH GREAT CARE, WHETHER THE SCHOOL'S OR SOMEONE ELSE'S

LISTEN WHEN YOU'RE TALKED TO BY ME

Teacher C regarded the 'whole child' as important and saw building on a specific child's experiences both in and out of school as the key to their full academic development. Hence appropriate multicultural education was necessary for a class with children of Caribbean heritage. Pupil-pupil relationships were important but trust was the most crucial element by which to create an environment where a child could and would share experiences. The last, Teacher E, believed that children were at school to work. The teacher's role, in relation to *all* children, was to promote a child's academic development by setting standards and helping as necessary. Personal development needed to be facilitated with empathy for children's concerns and plenty of opportunity for discussion and talk, to ensure that children were secure and that they behaved responsibly and reasonably.

While teachers' strategies for promoting the achievement of pupils of Caribbean heritage were influenced by their philosophies of learning, they may also have been affected by their perceptions of culture and of children's experiences of racism. The following two sections examine, firstly, their thoughts on culture and racism in greater depth and, secondly, the effect of these on the classroom models advocated.

Culture and Racism — Teachers' Perceptions

Two questions were especially helpful in exploring teachers' views about culture. The seventh question on the General Questionnaire focused on whether it is helpful for teachers to know about the culture of black children and black people in Britain. And question 9 asked teachers: 'When you think of white pupils, of pupils of Caribbean background and of Asian pupils, do you think they behave differently?'

It was clear that all the teachers thought it important to know about cultural backgrounds. Responses to question 7 were strongly expressed. Asked whether it is important to know about the culture of pupils of Caribbean background, the first teacher said: 'Oh yes!', the second: 'Yes, I think so, goodness me', the third: 'Absolutely', and the fourth: 'Yes, definitely'. The last replied quietly but with conviction: 'I'm sure it is'.

The first teacher had not referred to culture in response to question 3 but at this stage discussed the relevance of culture in the classroom to achievement. He expanded graphically on the effect on the confidence of pupils of Caribbean background of bringing in their culture and of enabling them to find out about 'the people who went before'. He stressed that culture should come in naturally and described how the 'children's eyes light up' when, for example, he included mangoes in a discussion about food.

The positive effect of bringing in culture was attributed to children's relating to their own — 'very rich' — culture, and also to countering the children's experiences of being excluded or ignored.

The views of Teacher B were similar. He thought a knowledge of culture was helpful and that it inspired the children partly, but not solely, by creating an interesting environment. Reflecting culture in the class-room was essential because of the existence of racism. The teacher believed that 'pupils will not learn unless they feel respected, welcomed and valued'.

Answers to other questions, including some on the Pupil Question-naires, indicated clearly that Teachers A and B believed that racism affected children's school and home experiences. Both thought that children of Caribbean heritage commonly underachieved compared with other groups, and that the curriculum content did not generally cater adequately for them. Both said that racial harassment occurred at their school and that they took it seriously and dealt with it. When a black child had reported an incident to one of these teachers, he had talked with the children involved, strongly reprimanded the name-caller and then dis-cussed the incident with the verbally abused child. The teacher's response was intended to show the child that she was valued and special, while encouraging her to shrug off of the incident: 'I know it's not nice to be called names. But look at it this way. We're all God's children. We have something to do. We were put in this world for a special reason. We just have to get on with it.'

Both these teachers mentioned the possible stereotyping of pupils by other teachers, in one case a pupil in his class and, in the other, three pupils, all of whom were labelled as naughty black children. Two other pupils might have been indirectly affected by racism, suffering undue hardships at home associated with racial disadvantages which affected the family and of which the pupils concerned were aware.

While these teachers held similar views about racism, they had differ-ent views about behaviour and its effects. The first was very clear that 'behaviour depends on the individual child' and that 'there is no particular way that black children behave'. He said: 'children of Caribbean heritage respond to the environment just as other children but sometimes home and school values don't coincide and this can confuse children who live between two cultures. Teachers need to know about culture because of this'.

In contrast, Teacher B expressed the view that it is not productive 'to deny that some Afro-Caribbean boys are very exuberant. They *are*. But there are ways to inspire and channel this.' The difference in behaviour attributed to this group of boys appeared to be partly linked with teacher stereotyping and the fact that 'if pupils are labelled as naughty black boys, they will behave badly'. But the teacher also appeared to believe in cultural differences, for 'if talking about children in the class who would be the most compliant, I couldn't claim that this would be the Afro-Caribbean boys, with some exceptions ...I'm not saying that black (i.e. of Caribbean background) kids behave badly but that they behave different-ly. Asian and white children are more compliant ... but with that they don't appear to be so questioning or so inquisitive'.

Teacher C had an almost personal and very positive view of the culture of families of Caribbean heritage, based on contact in the past few years with black friends and the pupils' parents. Like the first teacher, he saw culture as rich. That he was aware of racism emerged in talk about 'pressures on black pupils. Teasing happens, will happen. The pressures parents have had are also relevant.' But the main reason for reflecting children's culture in the classroom was not the valuing of culture per se, nor the awareness of racism, but his 'whole child' philosophy of learning.

Teacher D said that families of Caribbean heritage had very different perspectives on life and that both teachers and parents needed to be aware of this, teachers to avoid giving out the wrong signals, and parents because they need to know about the school. A knowledge of culture was important for effective home-school communication and helpful in making the classroom more interesting, a possibility which the teacher obviously appreciated. When asked about areas for self-development, the teacher had mentioned the need for books and artefacts, and had gone on to talking with enthusiasm about finding out more about the culture of children and ways to celebrate their backgrounds in the classroom. In the pupil inter-views, this teacher had referred to the positive image of the family brought in from home by one child, the involvement of another in the black community and of the opportunities of bringing in the pupil's background in the case of one child who was occasionally called racist names, because she talked so openly and positively about it.

For the last, Teacher E, a knowledge of culture appeared to be important primarily for listening to children's concerns, if and when they wanted to discuss them. His response to question 7 was that teachers need to be aware of children's backgrounds before they came to school, and possibly also of parental expectations and backgrounds. Nevertheless he was not at ease talking about culture or whether parents' experiences might be relevant. This was consistent with earlier comments about children's need for privacy, and the implication at various stages that what was important was the personal development of the pupil and that the teachers' role was

TEACHERS' PERCEPTIONS — CULTURE AND RACISM			
Teacher	Reasons for knowing culture (Q7)	Attitude to culture	Views on racism
A	Lifts children's confidence. Home/School values don't always coincide. Some children are confused by this.	Strong personal interest. Culture seen as rich. No difference in behaviour.	Many ways it affects children. Has negative effect on children.
B	Use to inspire children. Makes them feel valued, welcome.	'Happy to bring it in'. Difference in behaviour.	As for Teacher A.
C	Gives teacher an insight into the child.	Strong personal interest. No difference — behaviour.	Causes pressure on children. Families experience pressures.
D	Teacher won't give wrong messages in home/school links.	Interested in culture. Wants to know more.	Stereotyping as 'good at sports' can harm academic progress. Name-calling stopped, but less emphasis on victim's feelings than Teachers A,B,C.
E	If one knows backgrounds and experience, can empathise better with pupils' concerns.	Not really keen to pry into background of any child. Situations where Asian boys 'gang up'.	Not mentioned.

as a sensitive facilitator, empathiser and listener rather than expressing views or being nosey.

In answering question 9, Teachers D and E referred to situations involving Asian boys, and Teacher E remarked on their tendency to 'gang up'. These two teachers talked less about the pressures on children due to racism. Teacher stereotyping of pupils of Caribbean heritage as good at sports was mentioned by Teacher D but mainly in relation to monitoring to ensure that these pupils were given opportunities across the curriculum. The teacher also knew that name-calling occurred and condemned it but did not talk about how it might affect the pupils involved. This was true even in the case of one boy who had suffered quite considerable racism in another school.

Teacher E did not at any stage consider racism or negative experiences of children of Caribbean heritage due to 'race'. He talked about name-calling only when asked, and seemed content for pupils to handle it on their own. When he discussed one incident in which a pupil of Caribbean heritage got into a fight after being called racist names, the teacher simply said that the child had told the truth, which 'not many children would' and had been reasonable after the event.

In short, although this was a very small sample of teachers and, moreover, of teachers thought to be interested in meeting the needs of pupils of Caribbean heritage and aware of some of the issues, their perceptions of culture and of racism were far from uniform. There were different beliefs about the extent and nature of racism. Although all the teachers thought it important to know about the culture of children of Caribbean heritage, they had differing views about how it compared or contrasted with white British culture and the implications of this. And while most of the teachers recommended multicultural education, they did so for different reasons.

Teachers' Philosophies, Classroom Models

This section examines the classroom models which the teachers said applied in their classrooms and were useful for promoting achievement. The five different models are summarised in the table on page 99. The first column shows each teacher's starting point regarding the effects of 'race' and educational aims. The latter had several strands and only the key strand, given the highest priority by the teacher in the interview, is shown. All the teachers believed that it is helpful to know about children's culture so culture is not included in this column, though beliefs about the implications of culture come in as appropriate in other columns in the table.

Teacher A believed that racism had wide-ranging effects, encompassing among other things underachievement and name-calling, and that children of Caribbean heritage might suffer accordingly. The empathy this teacher showed with children who were verbally abused was obvious. A multicultural curriculum was seen as important for children to identify with and relate and respond to. Equally important in this classroom model was the teacher's educational goal of developing each child's academic potential to the full with specific strategies for monitoring and planning, geared to individual academic need, regardless of backgrounds.

Teacher B also put great stress on the potential effects of racism and hence on a curriculum which was multicultural. The educational aim most prioritised appeared to be to inspire children. This reinforced the need for a multicultural curriculum for children of Caribbean heritage and partly explained the teacher's emphasis on children doing their best. Teacher B revealed his belief in cultural differences, making references to influencing the pastoral care he thought necessary for 'channelling the energies of this group of children, rather than labelling them as naughty and so promoting anti-social behaviour'.

Teacher C considered educational aims to be predominant, and in particular the aim of providing security and promoting development based on the whole child. Nevertheless this teacher was aware of racism and its implications for the children in his care.

Racism had a much lower profile for Teacher D. He perceived monitoring achievement by children of Caribbean heritage across the curriculum as important, given the dangers of their being stereotyped as 'good at sports'. But his model was influenced primarily by the educational aim of motivating children through ensuring that tasks were interesting.

The experience of children because of being black and of Caribbean heritage was not regarded as of major consequence by Teacher E. He emphasised that educational goals for all children were the main priority.

TEACHERS' PERCEPTIONS, CLASSROOM MODELS				
Teacher	Starting Point	Pastoral Care	Content Taught Curriculum	Re Academic Outcomes
A	Pupils' experience can be negative. As a group are low profile, are not achieving fully. *Aim:* Develop potential.	Need for sensitivity, empathy.	Child-centred multicultural curriculum important — pupils respond relate, identify.	Organise for individual academic need.
B	Negative experience. Lower achievement *Aim:* Inspire children.	Labelling causes bad behaviour. Not naughty but behave differently. Questioning inquisitive. Channel this. Parental contact helpful in promoting good behaviour.	A relevant multicultural curriculum inspires. It promotes learning because it counteracts experience of racism as it values, welcomes, respects.	Be aware of group achievement. Children to know that *they* are expected to do *their* best.
C	Pupils are achieving. Pupils' experience can be negative. *Aim:* Secure. Whole development.	Relations depend on knowledge of child. Home school links helpful. No difference in behaviour.	Multicultural curriculum is important because it builds on experience.	Promote by building on experience.
D	As a group pupils are not fully achieving. *Aim:* Motivate through interest.	Working with parents is important especially as culture is different.	Multicultural curriculum is interesting to all. May be relevant to black pupils.	Monitor, across curriculum — ensure opportunities are there.
E	To promote learning — equal help, sanctioning empathy with concerns.	Important to be reasonable have sense of humour — to cope with life.	No mention of multicultural education.	Implicit that purpose of school is academic progress, good standard.

Researcher's Observations In the Classroom

This section describes first the findings from the earlier days in the five classrooms and then observations and analysis from the second part of the classroom research when observations were more focused.

Weekly visits to each class in the first fortnight were spent getting to know the classrooms and the underlying teacher philosophies and attitudes to pupils. First impressions were confirmed by later observations and, as will be seen, the reality of life in the classroom matched teachers' own views about their educational philosophy presented above.

In Teacher A's classroom, the emphasis was on teacher planning and concentration on the individual pupil. This was apparent as the teacher moved from table to table, focusing on support for the pupils, discussing concepts with them to further their understanding, praising or exhortating them to improve their work or behaviour, and correcting completed work.

All children received the same amount of teacher-attention while working at their tables, and each was encouraged to participate in the whole class discussions held in 'carpet sessions' when the class sat together. Also evident was the teacher's emphasis on children listening to one another, and the directness and regularity with which he exhorted children to think about and discuss standards expected of them.

Teacher B's emphasis on pupils doing their very best stood out. His personality was strong and his enthusiasm evident in organising and managing tasks done by children and his contact with them as individuals — whatever their background and whether or not they had problems. Teacher B was very welcoming to the parents who frequently came into the class after school, talking about their child's progress, and happy to listen when they talked about the child or about themselves.

Teacher C's interest in and ability to relate to the children and their cultural backgrounds was obvious, and especially so in whole class discussions when the class was sitting around the teacher on the carpet and had opportunities to talk about home. It was also apparent in the course of classroom activities as the teacher responded to children chatting about incidents outside the classroom. This teacher enjoyed stories from other countries, especially tales from families' countries of origin, and this was matched by equal enthusiasm on the part of the children. In effect, emphasis on knowing individual children, as Teacher C later told me 'in school and out', emerged almost immediately as an important aspect of this classroom.

All groups seemed to be treated equally by this teacher. There did not appear to be any difference in the quality and effectiveness of communication with different groups of children or with the parents who came into school.

There was often a lot happening in Teacher D's classroom, and he took interesting and different approaches, especially in promoting the enjoyment of stories. The children sometimes used a computer for their stories and they had an imaginative reading corner with a variety of books nicely laid out, and tapes for them to listen to.

Pupils appeared to have an unusually warm and trusting relationship with Teacher E. They talked among themselves about themselves and their backgrounds. While empathising with any out-of-school concerns and interests pupils wanted to discuss, Teacher E treated these as outside the main domain of the school. The implicit understanding was that *the* primary focus of his classroom was academic progress.

In the second part of this phase of the research, my observations became more focused and I scrutinised and compared the attention given to different groups, and examined the quality of teachers' interactions with pupils of Caribbean heritage. This seemed to me to be essential because published research had suggested that teachers may be hostile to pupils of Caribbean heritage and might give them more negative comments and punishment than they did to white pupils for similar behaviour (see chapter 2).

In each of the five classrooms, I devoted two separate periods of ninety minutes to checking this, applying an adaptation of the method developed by Brook for this purpose (Brook, 1991). This is a systematic method of focusing on the teacher for five minutes, followed by equal periods of time spent observing pupils at each of the tables in the classroom. What the teacher and pupils involved were doing was described. Teacher-pupil interactions were recorded and the tone used by teacher and pupil, and their body language during these interactions, scrutinised and noted.

These two ninety minute sessions showed that teachers spent about the same amount of time interacting with children of Caribbean heritage as with white pupils. Nor were there any apparent differences in the ways the five teachers responded to or interacted with children of these groups.

I continued my examination of the quality of interaction throughout the period of more focused observations when I researched six areas. The first was the teacher's 'gut' response to individual pupils, the second the apparent relative value attached to pupils of Caribbean heritage, both noted when recording verbal and non-verbal interactions between pupils and teacher. The teachers' acceptance of a child's, or her family's, feelings about their experiences was a third specific element.

A fourth, important element considered was whether the messages pupils of Caribbean heritage were receiving about academic goals were in any way shaped by different teacher expectations. Attention was paid to this when noting everyday teacher-pupil talk and the content of work set. Care was taken also when observing and recording the formal National Curriculum tests and teacher-pupil interaction during the tests.

The remaining two elements concerned culture. It seemed important to look at whether teachers were interested in, and confident about, finding out about cultural backgrounds different from their own, and to establish whether they valued cultures equally. Opportunities to explore this were scarce but were taken when they arose, as for example in discussions between teachers and parents, or when teachers commented spontaneously about individual pupils.

My research indicated that teachers' behaviour was generally the same towards individual pupils. They responded equally warmly and did not appear to act as if they perceived individuals of Caribbean heritage as in any way inferior to others.

Concerning the fourth area investigated, none of these teachers held lower expectations of pupils of Caribbean origin in their class than they did of the white pupils. This was most obvious during statutory assessments. Where pupils occasionally did less well than expected, teachers expressed their disappointment at children of Caribbean heritage as for others in this position, and were sad for the children who, as one teacher said: 'had not done themselves justice'.

Regarding the other three elements researched, the situation was less clear for three of the five teachers. Occasionally, they seemed to show less empathy for the feelings and problems of those of Caribbean background, including in situations not connected with 'race'. Teachers varied in the confidence they showed in finding out about 'Caribbean culture'. For all three, certain perceived aspects of culture were deemed less important or dismissed as difficult. And in times of extreme teacher stress, they seemed to have less empathy for situations concerning black pupils than for white pupils. Consequently, pupils of Caribbean heritage may have received some inadvertently negative messages about their backgrounds in some classes.

The more focused observations looked also at other aspects of the hidden curriculum such as the content of the taught curriculum, the sort of books available for children to read, the quality of teacher contacts with parents, and the messages conveyed by displays and the classroom environment (see page104).

With the exception of story writing, the taught curriculum did not appear to be truly 'multicultural' i.e. one permeated consistently by and informed by the culture of ethnic minority pupils. In most of the Spring term there was absolutely no sign of any multicultural content, apart from occasional accounts of home in children's diaries.

Some readers may not find this surprising in a term when teachers were noticeably under stress, weighted down by the time-consuming and additional duties of standard assessment tests. However I had expected something rather different from these more positive classrooms. Even the writing used for the national curriculum assessments uniformly ignored children's backgrounds, focusing instead on topics such as 'dinosaurs', 'witches', and 'a cold wet winter'. And in science work on weather, none of the classes appeared to draw on the children's Caribbean heritage.

Nevertheless, except for the teacher who appeared reluctant to bring any backgrounds into the classroom, some multicultural work did occur during the year, implemented as major projects and lasting several weeks. One class had done a project on Rastafarianism, another had done one on weddings of different sorts, and a third had focused on the Caribbean. And in the Summer term, another class did an intensive project on Africa, involving the whole year group.

Moving to stories, the five classrooms had books with which children from ethnic minority backgrounds might identify, although the scope and extent of these varied. In three classrooms, there were books with positive images of families of Caribbean heritage and culture, and the two others had stories with positive images mostly of other ethnic minority groups. The books were used by pupils, the class teacher reading to the class, and Section 11 teachers, who also brought in their own stories. The books

THE CLASSROOMS			
Books	**Curriculum Content**	**Ethos**	**Observation**
Wide range of stories with multicultural content, including large number with focus particularly relevant for pupils of Caribbean heritage.	i) Topic work not generally multicultural or even based on backgrounds. Class had done work on Caribbean in previous term. ii) Writing based on stories read while children were on carpet and these were frequently multicultural.	i) Classroom displays — Occasional images relevant to pupils of Caribbean heritage. e.g. children's work on Caribbean. ii) Teacher talk with pupils e.g. when on carpet — spontaneous references to Caribbean. iii) Some black parents attend assemblies.	Anansi stories, told when class sitting around teacher on carpet.
Some books relevant to pupils of Caribbean heritage.	Class had done work on Rastafarians in previous term.	i) Classroom not ideal for putting up displays. Relatively few. Posters from project on Rastafarians on wall. ii) Black parents welcome in classroom. Often talk with teacher when collecting children after school.	No input on backgrounds from class teacher while I was in classroom. Observed black teacher with class, reading poems by writers of Caribbean heritage.
Some books relevant to pupils of Caribbean heritage.	Over Summer term, focus of all work in year group was Africa.	i) In Summer term, displays on Africa. Previous terms, occasional specific relevant displays eg. poster of Louise Bennet. ii) Teacher talk with pupils in carpet sessions brought in ethnic minority backgrounds e.g. at time of Chinese New Year. iii) School emphasised multicultural focus.	Session on famous black women, focusing especially on Mary Bethune.
Stories from a range of cultures.	Work particularly relevant for pupils of Asian background. Project on weddings in previous term — all backgrounds.	i) Multicultural displays. ii) Black parents collecting pupils made welcome in classroom where often talked to teacher.	No opportunity to observe session relevant specifically to pupils of Caribbean heritage.

played an important part in conveying positive images to pupils, in a natural way and without any forced emphasis on multicultural issues.

The widest selection of books with a Caribbean/Black British focus was in Teacher A's classroom. They were routinely used, many read by the teacher to the class and used as a basis for children's story writing. Another of the teachers similarly used stories as a stimulus for story writing, and an Indian folk tale provided the basis for interesting work over several weeks. This story had specific relevance only for children of Asian background but conveyed the message to the whole class that non-white cultures were valued. Other aspects of the classroom ethos recorded and analysed were teachers' contact with parents of Caribbean origin, the focus of classroom displays, and the occasions when teachers' talk with the whole class brought in the backgrounds of the ethnic minority pupils.

Teacher-parent communication appeared good in all five classes. The frequency of contact appeared to vary from school to school. Some parents came in daily or weekly and others mainly to parents evenings. But it seemed as if parents of Caribbean heritage were generally welcomed and treated with respect.

Classroom displays, too, varied from class to class. In all cases, most of the displays had little relevance to the specific culture or backgrounds of children of Caribbean heritage. But as the table on page 104 shows, some positive material specifically relevant to children's backgrounds was displayed. Interestingly, the displays from projects which teachers perceived as having specific relevance to this group of pupils remained up for a relatively long time. This was true of the display on Rastafarians, the one on the Caribbean and a third on weddings, all projects done well before my research began. These appeared to be valued by children of Caribbean heritage, who commented on them to me at various stages.

The teachers very rarely talked about matters specifically connected to Caribbean heritage, except for Teacher A who referred spontaneously to the Caribbean on several occasions. Teacher C talked with children about what happened at home as a matter of course and family-related events with specific cultural connotations arose occasionally. For example, they talked about the Chinese New Year celebrations and one family's participation and the child concerned then brought in food to share with the class.

Thus, it would appear that for children of Caribbean heritage in these five classrooms, experiences connected with 'race' and cultural background were quite positive. There were no overtly negative situations associated with having a Caribbean background. There were specific and intensive short term projects which brought in Caribbean roots positively, even though the taught curriculum was not generally multicultural. There was a thread running through the general ethos of the classroom that all children were important regardless of their 'race'. And with the exception of occasional situations relating to a few aspects of culture and to teacher-sympathy for life experiences, children and families of Caribbean heritage were accepted and valued.

'Multicultural Education' for all Children

The next section examines the responses of children of Caribbean heritage to multicultural approaches but first three important points need to be made.

The first is that 'multicultural education' means different things to different people. It can mean the so-called 'Three S' approach (Samosas, Saris and Steel Bands) which has been strongly criticised for its ineffective and tokenistic representation of ethnic minority cultures. More commonly, however, it refers to educational philosophies ranging from what I call 'pure multicultural education' to 'antiracist/multicultural education'.

'Pure multicultural education' represents different cultures positively in the classroom, reflecting the lifestyles and experiences of ethnic minority groups within our pluralist British society and their countries of origin. The underlying assumption is that increased knowledge will foster understanding and harmony between different groups. 'Antiracist/multicultural education' incorporates also elements of antiracism, with a resultant challenging of prejudices at all levels and wide-ranging implications for school ethos, policy and practice.

Secondly, the reader needs to be aware of the lengthy debates which have taken place about whether a (pure) multicultural approach or an antiracist approach should be used. Critics of the pure approach argue that it is limited because it ignores racism, the power structures in society, and the consequent reality of institutional racism (see chapter 8 on institutional racism). Critics of the antiracist approach argue that it is extreme, 'political', and fosters confrontational and bureaucratic responses in its vocabulary and strategies. (For a more detailed discussion of debates see: Gundara, 1982; Hessari and Hill, 1989; Figueroa, 1991).

The third point is that although the focus in this book is on pupils of Caribbean heritage and their responses to, and need for, multicultural education I, like many others, perceive multicultural education as important for *all* children in Britain. Good education should provide a broad and balanced curriculum, relevant for the multicultural society in which we all live (Department of Education and Science, 1985). Moreover, some subjects cannot be taught adequately without a global 'balance'. A mono-cultural approach to geography gives children a biased view of certain countries, and history that concentrates only on one selected perspective gives an inaccurate picture of past events. Antiracism needs also to be incorporated since British society is both culturally diverse and racist (Figueroa, 1991).

However, this book is specifically concerned with children of Caribbean heritage so no attempt is made to examine the implications of multicultural work for white pupils, nor its consequences for the relationships between pupils from different ethnic groups. Nor are more general issues about the importance of multicultural education discussed. I shall include within the term 'multicultural' any work or resource which draws from, or discusses, minority cultures or people but I distinguish between 'pure multicultural' and 'antiracist/multicultural' approaches when this is relevant.

Multicultural Work Observed

I had hoped to be in the classrooms during activities planned by teachers to draw substantially on the specific backgrounds of pupils of Caribbean heritage. This was possible only in Teacher C's class which built work in the Summer term around a topic on Africa. Because of the difficulties of observing extensive work relating to backgrounds, two brief activities will be presented here.

Teacher A told an Anansi story quite spontaneously. He knew and loved the Caribbean. The children were familiar with Anansi stories from his storytelling and with the Caribbean from an earlier project on it, and they associated the stories with it. On this occasion, the class was sitting on the carpet with the teacher after a school assembly and responded enthusiastically when he asked if they wanted him to tell an Anansi story. The class, twenty-two of whom were white and with no Caribbean connections, participated with great enjoyment as the story was told. While the pupils of Caribbean heritage in the class revelled in the story, the quality of their participation was noticeably different to that observed on other occasions.

Like the white pupils, they normally participated in whole class sessions but, unlike them tended to do so only if the teacher directed questions at them or encouraged them to join in the class discussion. On this occasion and for the very first time in a carpet session, four of the five pairs of hands of the pupils of Caribbean heritage kept shooting up, spontaneously and without prompting, as they participated actively in the story.

One pupil, a very well behaved child, sat unusually straight and alert. Another sat sucking her thumb, something she had not done before. A third, a bright child, usually fully aware of the discussion though not necessarily appearing to concentrate on it, appeared very interested and, unusually, watched the teacher throughout the story. The fourth was listening, comfortable and relaxed, not sitting awkwardly as she often did. The fifth did not appear to be interested but nevertheless behaved quite differently to other occasions, not invading other pupils' space and not fidgeting or shaking her foot continually as she usually did. That the impact on these children of stories they connected with their roots was strong and positive was borne out in later informal interviews with them.

The session in Teacher B's class, where the Headteacher read poems by a Guyanese poet, John Agard, was equally revealing. The teacher talked about the Caribbean and its different countries, about the patois in which the poems were written, and then read a series of poems including High Heels, Hi Coconut and The Lollipop Lady.

The class was made up of eight white pupils, eight of differing Asian backgrounds, and thirteen of Caribbean heritage of whom I had observed seven for the case studies. The responses of the children of Caribbean heritage varied. Two were happy, interested and calm, but behaved much as usual. Another became unusually keen and focused, said very little, but concentrated much more intensely than usual.

Four other children were very different from their normal selves. One, who normally behaved well but did not take part in or relate to classroom sessions, sat bolt upright throughout. She put her hand up and asked questions or volunteered personal information, something I had never seen her do before. The second, who did not appear to be a happy child or to enjoy school and who sometimes seemed 'resentful', said little, but was unusually interested and obviously enjoying the session.

A child whose behaviour frequently caused concern, appeared slightly uncertain but very interested. She instigated a conversation with me afterwards, talking about the poems with obvious excitement, and spontaneously recounted various things she did at home. One very hyperactive pupil, young for her age, sat remarkably straight and still, concentrating for a prolonged period and, most revealing of all, apparently really involved for the very first time. She had an absolutely enraptured look on her face.

Since the poetry session was not with the usual teacher, and moreover was the with Headteacher, one can only draw tentative conclusions about the effect of initiatives building on children's roots. Nevertheless, my impression was that the high profiling of their Caribbean heritage partly explained these children's strong responses to this poetry session. Because of its novelty, the children were alert and ready to be interested, but they noticeably related and identified with the subject when the reading began. My impression was later confirmed by Teacher B who said in his interview that bringing in backgrounds had a noticeable effect on certain children of Caribbean heritage and that 'their behaviour and interest had changed noticeably for the better during a project on Rastafarianism in the Christmas term'.

The third observation, in a class with many pupils of Caribbean heritage and some of Asian background, was very different. This was part of several weeks' work on Africa, in the course of which the teacher and class had become quite involved in accounts of famous black people.

On this occasion, when the children were sitting together on the carpet, the teacher part-read and part-told the story of Mary Bethune, using a book called *Famous Black Women*. This class had twenty-nine pupils, six of them white, five of Asian background, and the remaining eighteen of Caribbean heritage. Typically, children of all the ethnic backgrounds in this class participated in discussions. But this time, all the discussion was by children of Caribbean heritage, including some who normally did not contribute or appear very interested. Children of other backgrounds appeared interested but it was as if they appreciated the fact that the black pupils had a particular need to think and articulate views on this topic.

The story was about black people and their resourcefulness and strength in the face of great odds. It told about slavery and some of the discrimination which followed. The teacher read about Mary Bethune and related that, as the youngest in her family, she was born just after the end of slavery so she alone of her family was born free and independent.

At this point, one pupil interjected 'So she was lucky!', and when the teacher went on to say that there were no schools for black people, asked 'How did she learn then?' The teacher described how black people who had acquired some learning shared it and helped others to learn so that everyone had a chance. The same pupil said, with obvious relief: 'Freedom. That's what it is.'

The other children were quiet but clearly engrossed in the question of equality and inequality. One pupil who had been sitting as if frozen, said suddenly 'Is this a true story?'. She later looked particularly thoughtful as the teacher read about the need to keep working and the problem of finding a place to stay, then interrupted the teacher again, saying 'There was nowhere blacks could go'.

When the teacher closed the book, a class discussion ensued involving many of the pupils of Caribbean heritage in issues about the unfairness of black children not having the opportunity to go to school, the consequences of this, and the effect of not being able to get jobs. The child who had spoken up during the story said hesitantly: 'But it's not so bad here' to which others replied 'Here there are black and white children in schools. It's good. All have a chance'. She then commented: 'It's friendly, white people and black people together'. The class did not go on to discuss the problems experienced in Britain, as they might have done in an anti-racist classroom.

When the discussion turned to slavery and the teacher asked what brought it to an end, a child who had a tendency to be disruptive but who was involved and engrossed in this session, responded quickly: 'It stopped because of some very brave people'. Other children joined in naming black people with great speed, 'Tacky, Sam Sharpe, Mary Seacole... A lot of brave people who fought against injustice'.

After discussing other aspects of the story the class settled down to their writing and again the children's involvement was enormous. While they wrote, they talked about the black people involved and discussed issues arising from the stories. They worked in small groups, some groups choosing a famous black person featured in previous sessions and others writing about Mary Bethune, talking with each other, not always getting their facts correct but displaying an enthusiasm and active involvement that I had not seen before.

This project indicated that even children as young as seven may be able to talk about overt and rather extreme cases of racism. The children appeared interested and able to take on the principles involved. One could argue that their tentative efforts to bring in situations closer to their own reality could have been channelled into current issues of prejudice in Britain and how these might be tackled to explore events familiar from their own lives. The fervour with which black figures were sought out and talked about indicated a real need for knowledge in this area.

What emerged from observing these three very different sessions was the noticeable effect of multicultural work that focused specifically on children's Caribbean roots. All the class responded well and enjoyed these sessions, but for pupils of Caribbean heritage the increase in involvement, interest and motivation was considerable and some of them behaved noticeably better than usual.

The session on Mary Bethune was particularly interesting and raises questions about whether even young children can and should take on some of the more sensitive issues to do with racism. None of the sessions described gave children the opportunity to talk about, reflect on and challenge issues of racism in Britain, problems which some may have experienced and which others, although with no first-hand experience, may have been aware of. In short, these teachers all used a 'pure multi-cultural' rather than an 'anti-racist/multicultural' approach (See page 106).

Successful Classrooms

What makes a school successful? A recent paper gives a synopsis of the different characteristics identified by HMI Reports and writings by educational researchers (Brighouse and Tomlinson, 1991) as being important. These include good leadership and management, clear aims translated into practice, an emphasis on high academic standards, a coherent and well planned curriculum, parental involvement and good relationships at all levels. For the classroom what appears to be important is that it should be orderly, firm, work-centred, relevant, structured, with tasks that are varied and intellectually challenging, with a climate of respect and positive feedback to and treatment of pupils.

What makes a good teacher? Teaching styles and the nature of tasks set are the relevant factors to consider. Ainscough and Muncey, in a twelve point analysis, note the importance of 'meaning', that tasks be challenging, ensuring progression, a variety of learning experiences and opportunities to choose. Also significant are positive atmosphere, consistency, recognition of the efforts and achievements of pupils, organisation of resources, cooperation and monitoring progress and providing regular feedback (Ainscough and Muncey, 1989).

These are certainly all important. The problem is that the lists are long and it is not immediately clear if and how one can prioritise. Most importantly, although some aspects may have particular relevance for the academic success of pupils of Caribbean heritage, no attempt is made to spotlight them. For our purposes then, it will be more helpful to return to the five classrooms in the research and see what light these can throw on models for promoting success.

The teachers' perceptions of their classrooms and how they helped to promote the achievement of pupils of Caribbean heritage were summarised in the diagram on page 91. I examined the notes from my observations and analysis to see if the reality of the classroom might differ from the teachers' own perceptions, and consequently made some additions and a few minor changes in emphasis. These are included in the final picture of the five classroom models set out on page 113. In every case, clear standards of work and behaviour and effective links with parents were also important elements.

Are all the models portrayed excellent and are they useful examples of good classrooms for pupils of Caribbean heritage? Analysis in the last section indicated that there were no major and overt disadvantages for pupils of Caribbean background in any of the five classrooms. The messages pupils received about their background were generally positive. There were a few 'grey areas', namely teacher empathy for pupils' experiences and the narrowness of the multicultural approaches adopted. But on the whole, I considered that the five classes were all environments in which pupils of Caribbean heritage might do well.

I hoped to use the analysis of classrooms in this chapter to identify classroom variables for a theory of achievement. The five models are all

CLASSROOM MODELS

Teacher A:

Specific awareness	— empathy, valuing — knowledge of Caribbean heritage
Individual potential	— focus — develop to the full
Opportunities for learning	— varied — interesting
Pupils	— listen to and respect others
	— take responsibility for self

Teacher B:

Each pupil	— emphasis on doing very best — respect for other pupils
Value pupils	— where behaviour is a problem criticise behaviour, not pupil. Stress problem can be resolved.
Environment	— to inspire, enthuse

Teacher C:

Build on whole child	
Use multicultural topics	
Environment	— stable, consistent, secure — relationships of trust — cooperative

Teacher D:

Environment	— interesting — offers opportunities
Backgrounds	— bring in when interesting
Opportunities	— ensure balance across curriculum
Monitor academic outcomes	

Teacher E:

Pupils' concerns	— privacy, empathy
All pupils	— promote personal development — important to be reasonable
Classroom goal	— academic development
Teacher role	— facilitator and provider of help

different from each other but each appears potentially helpful. It is impossible to compare performance in the classes and choose between the models, given the small sample size and the small numbers of pupils of Caribbean heritage in some of the classes. I have therefore looked at the models collectively and identified the following factors as of possible significance:

— Academic and behavioural expectations of this group of pupils equalling those of other pupils

— Valuing, respect, acceptance and empathy for individual pupils and their cultural and experiential background, whatever the teacher's perceptions of differences from white pupils

— Reflecting different cultures in the classroom

— An academic environment which is inspiring and stimulating, has clear objectives, and takes into account individual academic needs

— Routine assessment of achievement and its monitoring by ethnic origin

Since it is impossible to choose one or some of the five as more successful, it will be hypothesised that these are all key variables.

Summing Up

The schools selected for the research were all committed to meeting the needs of pupils of Caribbean heritage. Nevertheless, the five teachers differed considerably in their knowledge and views about the educational issues concerning this group of children.

Teachers generally believed it important to know about cultural backgrounds, but for significantly different reasons. And while three believed it essential to have a multicultural curriculum, their reasons were not the same. Some recognised racism as an important aspect of the children's lives. This did not necessarily influence any aspect of classroom practice, as was apparent in the case of one of the three teachers most aware of racism. For the other two, racism had a strong influence on how they viewed their interaction with children but was not discussed or articulated, and appeared to have a low profile.

Where specifically planned multicultural content was incorporated in the taught curriculum, as in four of the classes, it was not developed to enable children to discuss racism in Britain and appeared to employ a 'pure multicultural' rather than an 'antiracist/multicultural' approach.

The classroom models depended on the teachers' educational philosophy as well as their views about racism and their pupils' cultural backgrounds. In all five classrooms positive rather than negative messages were given, on balance, about backgrounds. Though the nature and degree of positive messages varied and could have been stronger and more sustained, it seemed to me that all five might foster achievement by children of Caribbean heritage and hence provided reasonable models of successful classrooms.

The next chapter looks first at the effect of 'race' and background on individual pupil experiences and achievement in the classroom, and then considers whether there was room for improvement in the five classrooms in the study.

Appendix for Chapter 6

General Questionnaire
('Black' used for 'of Caribbean heritage')

1. Do you think that, as a group and for whatever reason, black children underachieve?

2. To put this in a context for me, could you tell me a little about when and where you first had black children in your class?

3. We all want to ensure that black children achieve fully and to share ideas on how this can be done. Can you tell me what you do in your classroom to further this aim?

4. What do you think of as the two most important aspects of your classroom for all children?

5. How do the children in your class know what your expectations of them are, and your standards of work and behaviour?

6. As a teacher with black pupils, please tell me about any areas you would like to develop, given the time?

7. Do you think it is helpful for teachers to know about the culture of black children and black people in Britain? And about family backgrounds and experiences?

8. Could you name the three most rewarding children to teach in your class ? And the three most difficult?

9. When you think of white pupils, of black pupils, and of Asian pupils, do you think they behave differently?

10. Are there any comments you want to make?

Pupil Questionnaire

9. Looking at the achievement of X, do you think that the fact that she/he is black, and has a Caribbean background has/has had any relevance to her/his progress?

10. Do you think that X thinks of him/herself as black?

11. How does X feel about him/herself as a (black) British child, with Caribbean roots?

12. Has X ever been called names or teased because of being black?

Chapter 7

'Race' and Background in Positive Classrooms

This chapter explores how children's experiences in the classroom are affected by their being black and of Caribbean heritage. As discussed in chapter 3, effects can be positive or negative, the negative arising from teachers' lack of knowledge of aspects of Caribbean culture or from discrimination based on 'race' or culture. Such effects will be described as the consequence of children's 'race' and background.

In this chapter, the data collected on 'race' and background experiences is used to extend the analysis of factors affecting the achievement of pupils of Caribbean heritage. The chapter ends by looking at the implications of this research for some current debates regarding the education of such pupils.

Data on 'Race' and Background Experiences

There were only a few occasions during the classroom observations when Caribbean backgrounds or 'race' came in explicitly and, when they did, I took great care to make detailed records. If pupils mentioned their family, or aspects of 'race' or cultural backgrounds in their writing or drawing, it was carefully noted. I recorded the children's responses to storybooks

117

relating to ethnic minority backgrounds. The multicultural projects or whole class sessions described earlier provided useful data, as did visits by black people to the classroom, and I made a point of observing the reactions of individual pupils.

Outside the classroom, opportunities arose for listening to pupils or participating in talk which clarified pupil experiences, for example conversations about foods eaten or multicultural displays, references to family and school activities and, occasionally, teasing or name-calling. While showing empathy with the feelings expressed, I tried to appear as detached as possible, following the course of the conversation rather than steering or influencing it.

Occasionally, 'race' and background issues were explicitly raised. In the second interview with the pupils, I deliberately explored their responses and feelings. Interviews took place outside the child's classroom and I told her/him: 'I'm working in lots of different schools, finding out about things children do. One of the things that I'm particularly interested in is what children today learn about other countries.' Then I asked what their class had learnt about different countries. At the end of the interview, I asked them about their experiences at school and about teasing and name-calling.

Very occasionally when I was with the pupils, I would take opportunities to increase the chance of pupils discussing 'race' and background issues. When I read to children or shared books with them, I might deliberately choose a story with possible relevance to the child's Caribbean/black British background. I might draw attention to displays relating to children's backgrounds, perhaps by asking which class had been responsible for the display. I always took care to phrase questions as openly as possible so as not to influence the responses, and I tried to participate and empathise with pupils, occasionally asking for clarification but trying not to steer the discussion.

When observing pupils, I paid attention not only to overt behaviour and verbal communication but also to non-verbal communication and body language. Because of the dangers of misinterpretation, I kept careful and detailed notes, considered different interpretations of the observations, and sought alternative explanations when necessary. Clues were accepted as firm evidence only if they proved consistent with other clues and if all pieces of the jigsaw fitted. Some children's responses to me appeared to reflect an awareness of my 'race' and background, and I was particularly careful when interpreting such responses. I regularly reviewed the emerging picture of the child, reminding myself of the need to keep an open mind and to be flexible and able to revise my emerging perceptions.

Halfway through the period of collecting data on the pupils, I interviewed the five class teachers about each pupil. Since it was important that the teacher's perceptions did not influence mine, the teacher interviews were put aside until I had completed and analysed my observations. I did however consider the views of the advisory teachers who had contact with some of the children and their families outside school.

Case Studies

The field work focused on the twenty-five case study pupils, fourteen girls and eleven boys. Ten of them are described below, illustrating processes through which 'race' and background impinge on children's experiences in the classroom. To increase confidentiality in such a small sample, the gender of pupils is not revealed. Personal pronouns are restricted to she and adjectives to her or their, even when the pupil concerned is a boy.

The descriptions of individual children indicate the way that data collected were used to form a picture. They highlight the difficulties in coming to conclusions about some children and the need continually to review and keep an open mind. Where teacher interviews later clarified my analysis, supplying additional information and adding another piece to the 'jigsaw', the relevant points from the teacher interview are included here. The first examples are of pupils who had negative experiences at school because they were black and of Caribbean heritage.

Pupil One appeared motivated and reasonably interested in carrying out tasks set. This child worked well, at a table where all the children were judged to be particularly able. In spite of good performance and my impression of a settled and balanced seven year old there was something, extremely difficult to pin-point, which suggested that things were not as straightforward as they seemed and that the pupil felt uncertain. Moreover, something about the child's body language made me ask myself whether I was being weighed up. The child seemed watchful and careful, interested in me and, I felt, very aware of my 'colour' but unsure about me and how to relate to me.

After subsequent observations and conscious efforts to observe very carefully and openly, the initial impressions persisted and with little clarification. The pupil's behaviour was excellent and although a bit of a loner and with no obvious regular friends, there appeared to be no obvious difficulty in relationships with peers. When interviewed, she mentioned two others in the class as special friends, both of them black.

Unsure whether to discount my first impressions, I decided to use shared reading to try to get closer. The child chose a book called *Mufaro's Beautiful Daughters*, about two African princesses. We looked at a picture of one of the princesses and I exclaimed 'What a beautiful brown skin she has'. This proved to be a turning point in our relationship. A fleeting reaction, like relief, was evident. Thereafter, the child frequently wanted to be with me and read with me and, increasingly, evidence accumulated which suggested that she lacked confidence and that this was rooted in her awareness of racism.

After a black teacher visited the class and spontaneously told them about Caribbean foods, Pupil One talked to me about the food at home. A child of Asian origin standing nearby whispered that they ate roti and dhall at home. When I asked why the whispering, we had a discussion of different foods, the differences between backgrounds, and about name-calling at school. Both children's uncertainty about talking about their cultural heritage was clearly apparent.

Through talking with these two children in the classroom, at dinner and at playtime, a clearer picture emerged of the case study pupil. She was very clever, advanced in reading and good at maths, but not articulate and as yet without the interpersonal and communication skills for making and enjoying friendships. She seemed to suffer from an awareness of prejudice which, acutely felt, she found difficult to talk about.

It often appeared that the other child took the lead in the growing companionship, and, although only just becoming fluent in English, was expressing events or feelings for them both. A bond grew between them, fostered by the problems which they had in common: their difficulty in speaking English and their coming from ethnic minority backgrounds and so possibly being regarded as 'black and inferior' by prejudiced people.

As I grew to know Pupil One better, I began to think that my initial suspicions about the response to me might have been affected by our difference in skin colour and the fact that I was considerably less dark.

Interestingly, towards the end of the summer term, Pupil One wrote 'I have nice skin.' For some children, this could be taken at face value, but in the case of this pupil, and in the context of other evidence suggesting a great sensitivity to any possibility of hostility based on being dark, my perception is that this was a cry for reassurance from the teacher with whom the child felt secure.

To summarise, it seemed to me that while being in the classroom was a generally positive experience for this pupil, being black added a very real and negative dimension that reduced confidence. For Pupil One, experiences due to 'race' and background took the form of awareness of prejudice and the hostility associated with it, felt very intensely, just below the surface, and all the more painful because of the child's shy personality, strong feelings and as yet undeveloped skills for making friends and expressing feelings. It seemed to me that achievement was and would continue to be affected. For although performing very well, among the the best in the class, the uncertainty and inability to make friends and participate in a group was preventing optimum achievement.

Pupil Two appeared to have a more generally negative experience of the classroom. While at least part of this seemed due to the child's 'race' and background, it was difficult to obtain clues which could help confirm or reject this possibility. This was a child one could describe as 'not happy'.

In the first few weeks of observation, I spent time listening to reading, encouraging talk and listening carefully, and looking at the pupil's writing and drawings. The child normally looked lethargic but would light up and smile on seeing me. The stories the child wrote contained incidents which were violent or upsetting. Indeed, they gave the impression of being by someone who had suffered a great trauma.

As the observations progressed I could see that the child had special friends and did occasionally relax and work well, but my impression of trauma continued and strengthened. Often the child seemed weighted down, finding it difficult to concentrate, and occasionally seemed to seize up and be unable to think. Pupil Two took great care over presentation, sometimes to excess but this did not appear to be the cause of her difficulties. Nor did the problems over concentration appear associated with late nights and tiredness, or with inappropriate tasks or other likely explanations.

She appeared more relaxed with me, and noticeably so with the black teacher who sometimes worked in the room. This is not to suggest that the child disliked or appeared ill at ease with the class teacher — indeed the teacher was clearly respected and trusted. But there was a different quality of relationship with me, a black person, and also with the black teacher — something warmer, more accepting and secure. The child was evidently aware of the other three black pupils in the class, occasionally calling out to them, or looking at them across the room, as if watchful and protective.

Unfortunately, I had no chance to observe Pupil Two when engaged in multicultural activities and the second interview, helpful in raising issues, kept being delayed by unforeseen events at school. Occasionally useful information came to light in the first interview with a pupil but not in this case. Pupil Two had talked easily in the (first) interview about work, and about being good at 'playing conkers and reading stories' and liking 'playing games like What's the time Mr. Wolf and Tig and Snakes and Ladders' she had also talked about what was done at home, but had not mentioned family roots or anything else related to background.

Only when I interviewed the teacher about Pupil Two did a vital clue emerge which made sense of the observation. When asked how the child felt about being black, the teacher replied 'Very aware. She can be very defensive... when she first came into the class, when there was free writing, she would write 'I am black and I am glad." It emerged that the child had come into the class from another school where she had been called racist names in the playground, and had suffered behavioural problems.

This made sense of my impression of trauma gained from Pupil Two's writing and behaviour and her greater security and identification with black people. It seemed likely that writing 'I am black and I am glad' indicated considerable insecurity about identity and a need for reassurance due to her traumatic experiences of harassment. It is possible that Pupil Two's lack of concentration and her other problems also had their origins in the trauma and racial harassment in the previous school, and that the underachievement evident in the unacceptable quantity and quality of her work compared with that of younger pupils in the class, was due to continuing emotional problems.

Pupil Three, newly in year two, was initially observed in a class of younger children. This pupil appeared to do little if any work on the tasks set. Although not overtly disruptive, there was a lot of messing around — throwing rubbers, walking about, going to the toilet, and talking to others, rather more extreme behaviour than that of most pupils. In the new class, the child worked much more consistently and effectively, concentrating more and behaving reasonably well. The child had clearly been performing well below potential in the previous class.

Pupil Three had achieved almost nothing and yet all my observations indicated a very clever child. She was very alert, taking everything in, and quick at picking up ideas and concepts. Even when appearing not to be focusing or concentrating, discussions revealed that she was fully aware and absorbing everything.

Moreover, this pupil appeared to have wide interests. Sometimes I saw her playing with her sister in the playground. There were books at home, about which the sister talked and both were interested in them. Pupil Three tended to be quiet but when action rather than talk was required, showed great skill and quick thinking, for example in doing some mathematical puzzles. At a school assembly at which a range of musical instruments were described and played, the child was unusually enraptured by the talk and music and sat quite still, absorbed by the experience.

Talking more with both siblings, I gathered that the family was a caring one, with a closeness reflected in the unusually strong relationship between the two children.

The general picture developing was of a very quick and clever child, from a close and secure family, who had performed far below potential before transfer and who appeared unformed and unaware of self and strengths, and was likely to be easily swayed by events. After transfer, behaviour and performance improved, and concentration, confidence and purpose increased steadily. But there was a lot of catching up to do and so underachievement continued.

Several points emerged in my discussions with the pupil, teachers and her sister, in which 'race' and background appeared to figure. The most relevant to the pupil's experience in the previous class, was that the child had been stereotyped as a naughty black child at an earlier stage in school and that this labelling had affected her behaviour. This was consistent with the differences in observed behaviour in the two classes and with my impression of a clever but somewhat unformed child, absorbing environmental clues like a sponge and acting accordingly.

The level of this child's academic attainment, then, had been very low initially in comparison to her potential, and seemed attributable to previous experiences in school arising from her 'race' and background. The initial level of underachievement was so great that even after the main causes had been removed by transfer to the new class, full potential was still not being attained.

Pupils Four and Five, considered next, are very different. Both appeared to be reasonably happy and had positive experiences in the classroom. They played and worked well with others, and did the tasks set by teachers quietly and thoughtfully. Both were quite polite, related well to adults and had a good rapport with other children.

Pupil Four was imaginative and unusually gentle, acutely aware of feelings, as the stories written showed. They often featured families and feelings and descriptions of adults and children that included the phrase 'was happy'. My initial feeling, justified or not, was that the pupil identified with me, that my colouring, similar to the child's, was a factor, and that in the contact with me, the child was alert, as if seeking something out.

This view appeared to be confirmed when Pupil Four was alone with me and reading to me for the first time. Suddenly and unexpectedly, the child began to tell me that her mother had lived in Jamaica as a twelve year old. Although the child did not know much about Jamaica, her interest and enthusiasm were obvious.

Later, when asked during the interview about learning about other countries, the same interest and enormous enthusiasm was evident. The pupil told me at length about what the class had learned about Africa, talking far more quickly than usual, almost breathlessly, when recounting different aspects and details of the project. It was as if a great need was at last being fulfilled, by the focus and scope of the project which the class had recently begun.

I had observed Pupil Five carefully from the start because staff had told me, early on in my research, about her extreme behaviour at the beginning of the school year. When brought to school, she had screamed and had had to be restrained, and reassured and helped to settle. By the time of my observations in the Spring and Summer terms, the child was behaving normally and consistently, seemed reasonably happy and motivated and was relating well to children and adults. This pupil was always polite with me and on discovering that I came from the Caribbean and had worked there, seemed keen to talk and was particularly inquisitive about the Caribbean.

During the second informal interview when we talked about other countries, Pupil Five's responses were unusually thoughtful in comparison with others in the same class and with the answers given by pupils in other classes. The child talked at length about the work done in a previous term focusing on the Caribbean, and the sorts of things the class had learnt, saying that it 'sounds good', and expressing a wish to visit a grandmother who still lived in the Caribbean. When asked whether it is a good idea for children who do not have family there to learn about the Caribbean, the child said 'Yes. They like hearing about it. They like the same things and other things', and volunteered that 'I'd like to know about people from the Caribbean. I haven't heard a lot. I'd like to hear more because I can see what people there have been doing.'

During an interview with me, the teacher who had described the problems experienced in the Autumn term, tentatively asked whether this pupil could perhaps be like another child, a boy, who also had one white parent, was in the class in a previous year and had had an inner feeling of not knowing where he belonged. Could some of the early difficulties with Pupil Five, i.e. stormy tantrums and problems when settling in, be due to the uncertainty about identity shown by the pupil in the previous year? The teacher's comments were completely consistent with the picture I had built up from my observations, of a thoughtful and independent child actively seeking information about roots.

Indeed it seemed to me that Pupils Four and Five both needed to know about their roots but that different manifestations of this basic factor were reducing their achievement. Pupil Four seemed to have a very strong potential drive which was repressed in favour of a clear and compelling need for discovering roots and history. Whereas the response of Pupil Five was initially unacceptable behaviour that meant that little work was done.

Pupils Six and Seven also appeared to find education building on their own backgrounds important. Both pupils were discussed in chapter four. (See first and second pupils described in group 2 on pages 64, 65.)

These children were very well behaved and worked consistently but it seemed to me that their motivation for working was considerably less than it could have been, mainly because of a lack of involvement with the work they did.

Work did not arouse Pupil Six's interest and imagination. She worked reasonably well and happily but without any real drive or spark. This contrasted with behaviour in conversations with me which related to people, events or themes to do with home, when she became very animated and inquisitive and interested in any contributions I could offer.

Pupil Seven appeared to be quite disinterested in work done in the classroom. Yet when reading with me, and talking about family and family concerns, the child was quite transformed, displaying a sense of humour, articulateness, and spontaneity in questioning and interpreting situations. During a multicultural session described in the last chapter, Pupil Seven's involvement and enthusiasm was apparent. It appeared to me that this pupil, normally very quiet and almost invisible, worked methodically in the classroom because this was expected by home and school, but that the home world was so completely different that the child did not generally relate to tasks set at school.

Pupil Eight: The pupils described so far all had experiences associated with 'race' and background which were primarily negative or were somehow not as fulfilling as they should have been, but for a few pupils in the case studies, experiences included positive as well as negative ones. One such pupil is of particular interest, since it proved difficult to unravel the way that 'race' and background came into her school experiences. Early on I had been told that this pupil had been called names and had become very distressed. Many children are upset by being called names, but the reaction seemed unusually strong and made me wonder whether Pupil Eight had had previous painful experiences arising from background or had low self-esteem.

Pupil Eight was always glad to see me, greeting me warmly, making a good deal of eye contact, and seeming to relate to and identify with me. Initially I felt that this was to do with my links with the Caribbean, although I had no evidence. The child's response to name-calling and to me seemed to warrant careful investigation. I sought possible explanations in as open and detached a way as possible, with completely unexpected results, unlike any that I could have predicted.

In the classroom, she would work at a table with the same three close friends — all white — talking occasionally but consistently carrying out the task set, quietly and happily. All drew beautiful pictures, taking great care and doing so before writing. They talked together about their work and frequently produced very similar work.

In the playground, the child would usually be with one or more of these friends but sometimes also with younger pupils, as once observed sitting in a circle playing 'eating fish and chips'. Although Pupil Eight's closest friends appeared to be these white pupils, when the children lined up, when coming from assembly to class for example, the child always came in with at least two of the other black pupils, not necessarily the same ones, and she also clustered with other black pupils in the playground in spite of the relatively small proportion at the school.

In the first interview, Pupil Eight was trusting and confident, showing me a tray of work, and sharing it with me. She enthused quietly about a number of things and was noticeably positive in approach. Talking about a playgroup at an Afro-Caribbean Centre that she attended before coming to school, led naturally to her volunteering information about family and roots and the fact that the family had been to the Caribbean. It seemed increasingly unlikely that this child had low self-esteem. Rather, she had strong and warm feelings about her Caribbean roots and heritage. It was also evident that her family were positive about their background, deriving great satisfaction from keeping in touch and seeing it as important to visit the Caribbean. A chance meeting with Mum, when she brought the child to school one morning, added another piece to the jigsaw, as Mum saw her child as well able to cope with name-calling and able to talk about it.

A number of events, including a semi-formal interview with a teacher who often worked with the class, added the final clues which made everything fall into place. The teacher gave a picture of a shy or cautious pupil, very careful, afraid to make mistakes, being held back by her cautiousness and certainly not performing to her full potential.

Reading with and interviewing the pupil — explicitly raising issues of 'race' and background — expanded my earlier picture to one of a child whose world was firmly located in the culture of the local black community and its Caribbean links. Her world gave the pupil security and it was familiar and safe. Talking about name-calling, Pupil Eight's response demonstrated her strong principles about fairness and justice, and her combination of trust that wrongdoings would not be sanctioned by those in control and anger that individuals could carry out unjust actions.

Summing up, being a black British child with Caribbean roots was a crucial part of Pupil Eight's life experience. Being black meant that some experiences were negative, for example name-calling and other illustrations of racist ideology. But feelings and responses to these derived not from poor self-esteem but from strong feelings about injustice. The pupil benefited enormously from being in a class threaded through with positive references to the Caribbean and this almost certainly fostered her confidence.

Nevertheless, Pupil Eight was underachieving. Drawings were excellent but the accompanying written sections were brief, unimaginative and in a repetitive and uninteresting style. This contrasted with her fluency and interest, and above all, her confidence when focusing on things to do with the Caribbean.

I concluded that Pupil Eight was underachieving, due partly to a sensitive and cautious personality when exposed to an unknown and hence alarming world. Any resolution would probably depend on being in a school environment which included curriculum content founded cohesively and solidly on Caribbean roots. This would enable the pupil to take the risks involved in moving out to work with less familiar and secure content.

Pupils Nine and Ten: This section would not be complete without descriptions of pupils for whom 'race' and background experiences had no effect on their achievement. They tended to be pupils whose classroom experiences associated with 'race and' background were positive, mainly because of a positive sense of self associated with strong family valuing of roots. Among them were Pupils Nine and Ten, two of the three group 1 pupils described on page 63, very high achievers and so of interest in view of the lack of research on such pupils. The very different responses of these pupils make their accounts particularly interesting.

Pupil Nine was a bright child, with extensive interests, ideas and initiative whose Caribbean roots were an important part of her life. Even in a classroom which tended to ignore backgrounds this rootedness added positively to experiences. It came naturally into conversations with other black pupils in the class, usually instigated by this pupil, and the interest in background added a special quality to the child's classroom experiences. However although the very positive valuing of roots reinforced the child's confidence and enhanced the range of interests, it did not seem to me to be significant in fostering her outstanding achievement. This appeared to arise from the pupil's confidence, unusually strong self-motivation and her wide interests. These performance-enhancing factors seemed due, in turn, to a combination of ability, good parental academic support, and a history of success.

Pupil Ten, also from a supportive home which valued background, did not appear to be curious about roots nor to regard them as a personal priority. Nor was school work so regarded. Although very bright and working well and effectively, discussions suggested that the pupil was not particularly interested in classroom work, but was simply doing what was expected rather than being self-motivated or working for personal satisfaction. The things that made Pupil Ten light up and talk in an animated way appeared to be friendships and activities with friends and the everyday happenings to do with them.

The more overtly negative experiences associated with being black, such as verbal abuse, did not affect this pupil, who was respected and looked up to by friends. Nor did the covert signs of racism in society, which this quick, alert and clever pupil might have noticed, appear to have any effect. This was partly because of the child's preoccupation with friends rather than issues or principles, and partly because of being very secure, special and valued, not only at home but at school by friends and the teacher.

Analysis of Case Studies

All the twenty-five case studies were developed fully. Since all could not be described here, I chose to describe the ten histories that reflect a representative sample of the processes involved and the conclusions to be drawn from the whole sample.

What emerged clearly from the full set of case studies was how the 'stories' of the children differed. Children's encounters with differences in 'race' and background, in and out of school, and their experiences in the classroom varied considerably. Some pupils had positive experiences and were confident and knowledgeable about their backgrounds, which they valued and felt secure in. Others were not really interested or found the connection painful. Where this happened, the intensity of children's feelings differed: some felt angry or upset and confused, others more philosophical and accepting.

The nature of encounters was not the same for all pupils. Some had absorbed messages implying that people who are black and of Caribbean origin attract hostility, and a few were aware of shades of prejudice. Others appeared to be indirectly affected, their families suffering additional hardships attributable to the effects of racism in society. The pupils conscious of this were angry about the situation and its unfairness.

Some had had more personal experiences of a negative kind, overtly through being called racist names at school, or less directly through stereotyping as naughty black children. Others showed an awareness of being different and a need to search for roots and discover their history.

Other children felt secure in the black British world they were familiar with, but their reactions varied in the less familiar world of school. Some did not relate, or were not involved, while others felt exposed and at risk.

Yet others, unconscious of differences that existed between home and school, found school confusing and difficult to handle because of these differences. One such case study was described (see the group 6 pupil, pages 67, 74).

In addition to the variation in intensity of feelings and the nature of encounters, there were differences in the consequences for pupils. Children's confidence, behaviour and motivation were affected. But the key variable, processes and patterns differed between pupils, and the personal and social skills of a child influenced and in turn depended on their individual reactions.

In spite of the variability observed, it is clear that a good many pupils had in common classroom experiences associated with 'race' and background which were at worst negative and at best unfulfilling. This is not to say that these pupils were desperately unhappy in school, but these experiences had notable consequences for the children's confidence, behaviour, and motivation, so had a potentially harmful effect on their achievement.

'Race', Background and Achievement

The case studies suggested that although children's experiences arising from their 'race' and background were not the only influence on achievement, they played an important part. When the analysis was extended to look at the impact on achievement, two patterns emerged for the twenty-five children.

Some children had negative experiences, fifteen wholly so. Another four had both negative and positive experiences but the overall effect was harmful. This meant that for nineteen pupils the effects appeared to depress achievement.

For the second group of six pupils, the situation was very different. Three pupils appeared not to have any experiences, either negative or positive, attributable to their being black and of Caribbean heritage. One of these three was described in Group 8 in Chapter 4, as of major concern to the teacher, and performing very poorly. The second was Pupil Ten described earlier in this chapter, a high achiever with specific and personal priorities in which experiences arising from her Caribbean background played no part. The third was confident and had a wide range of interests but, like Pupil Ten, had specific and personal priorities unrelated to background.

For the remaining three, whose experiences seemed to be enhanced by factors associated with their Caribbean background, this seemed of little consequence for their levels of achievement/underachievement. In two cases it was their extensive interests and the fact that they were very supported at home and school that appeared to be the key to their achievement. One was Pupil Nine described earlier. The third was a confident pupil whose progress was hindered by very poor behaviour and her confidence, evident interest, knowledge and confidence about identity seemed irrelevant both to behaviour and achievement.

In designing the research, I hoped that the light thrown on the processes involved in pupils' achievement would help to identify relevant factors and develop a new and better model to explain achievement. Gender is one potential factor — this is discussed first.

There may have been minor differences between boys and girls in the specific nature of their encounters with 'race' and background. Stereotyping, for instance, affected boys more than girls, and their consequent disruptive behaviour reduced their achievement. Interestingly, there were

131

no boys in the second group i.e. those for whom 'race' and background experiences were entirely positive. This suggested that girls have a better chance of not picking up or responding to negative influences. In effect, boys appear to be more vulnerable. Since the sample is small, one cannot say whether these are typical gender differences or whether they arise from special characteristics of the pupils in the sample.

Girls did not appear to have a greater chance of success than boys. There were underachievers among the girls in my case studies and, for many, their experiences arising from 'race' and background were a contributory factor. Indeed, the relevant factors appeared to be similar to those for boys, i.e. lack of motivation, unsatisfactory on-task behaviour, other forms of poor behaviour and lack of confidence. The case studies suggest therefore that the underachievement of pupils of Caribbean heritage cannot be seen as restricted to boys.

Next I examined the results from the case studies for implications about children's confidence, valuing of roots, behaviour, and achievement.

Many pupils appeared to me to be confident, fifteen in all. For nine of these, their interviews and conversations revealed a strong and positive family projection of roots. One noticeable characteristic that they had in common was the way that they talked about adult members in their family with great warmth and interest. All clearly felt a strong family bond.

Nine of the fifteen (including some but not all of the nine with a strong projection of roots), were generally well-behaved though not all of them worked well on task. The remaining six displayed generally poor behaviour and, for three pupils, negative factors such as racist stereotyping or their own confusion over home/school differences were, or had been, the dominant causes. Thus, confidence and a valuing of roots do not necessarily indicate that 'race' and background experiences will not hinder achievement.

The remaining ten of the twenty-five pupils seemed insecure or lacking in confidence, some especially so. Awareness of racism or a lack of confidence about identity, seemed to play a part in this, sometimes a major part and sometimes interweaving with other influences to exacerbate insecurity. Interestingly, these pupils did not talk willingly about their family or their roots.

It is suggested, very tentatively, that children's valuing of roots along with their security within the family can contribute to their confidence and to achievement — but not in every case. For some children, such conditions may help to promote confidence but behaviour may nevertheless be poor for reasons associated with negative experiences. For other children, lack of confidence may be the problem. The effect of children's personal and social skills can also be potential influences on their achievement.

The above variables can be incorporated in a model of achievement but the analysis of the case studies in this chapter and chapter 4 suggests that this should be done at different levels. At one level are factors involving pupils' encounters with differences in 'race' and background, for example, the direct and indirect racism experienced by the child, differences between home and school, and the value put by the family on valuing identity. The value placed by the school on children's cultural backgrounds and the practices of teachers and others that attempt to counteract racism, considered in chapter 6, are also relevant factors.

At another level, there are variables relating to the child. These embrace their personal and social skills, confidence, behaviour, motivation and the attitudes to school. At yet another level are the variables which have a direct influence on academic outcomes i.e. ability, attainment to date, and on-task behaviour

A model incorporating these variables is set out in the final chapter. A few points are noted here. First, the case studies suggest that the effect of 'race' and background experiences on pupils of Caribbean heritage depends on how each child reacts. The impact cannot be predicted and varies from pupil to pupil. Moreover, the process does not follow a single pattern. A combination of lack of confidence and poor behaviour can cause poor performance and minimal output. In another child, lack of confidence might cause poor behaviour and this reduce concentration and output. For another, trauma associated with racial harassment may be the trigger that reduces concentration. And there are many other possibilities.

Secondly, given the lack of uniformity in the processes involved and the qualitative nature of many variables, it may be difficult to formulate or test a quantitative model of achievement.

Teachers' Perspectives

The interviews showed that teachers had thought about issues connected with 'race' and background. Their reasons for knowing about the culture of groups of children and for multicultural education, summarised in the tables in chapter 6, fit with most of the factors revealed by the case studies in this chapter. However, the teachers had not connected them with the experiences of individual pupils. Their responses to the question on the relevance, if any, of a child being black and of Caribbean background, were spontaneous and occasionally seemed to draw on generally held views about the education of ethnic minority pupils rather than on their knowledge of the individual pupil, as shown by their responses described in chapter 4. This section re-examines these responses in the light of my perspective on the twenty-five case study pupils.

Two of the teachers each identified one of their pupils as benefiting from a positive image of her roots. The underlying assumption was that children who are confident about their identity will participate more actively in the classroom. The two children concerned did not appear to me to participate any more actively because they valued themselves and their background.

Language was said by three teachers to be a cause of underachievement by three pupils. My observations showed that, in each case, language in its widest sense, including spoken English and articulateness, was a factor but that other factors were equally or more important.

The variable identified for certain pupils and the direction of its effect agreed with my perspective, but the relative importance attributed to it did not. In one case the teacher appeared completely unaware of the intensity and severity of the effect of racism on a child. In several other cases, teachers failed to identify some of the key variables.

Sometimes the teachers' statements appeared to be contradicted by my observations. For two children said to be affected positively, I had evidence that the reverse was true. It was suggested that a pupil with one white parent felt inferior in comparison with black friends, a perception in no way supported by my observations.

Overall, the teachers' perceptions of the effect of children's 'race' and background was very different from that obtained from my analysis. Teachers thought that for fourteen pupils, their 'race' and background was not relevant or had a positive effect. This contrasts with my own findings

RACE, BACKGROUND AND ACHIEVEMENT		
EFFECT	Teacher's View	My View
Negative	10	19
Both	0	0
Positive	4	0
No effect	10	6
Don't know	1	-
Total	25	25

that only six pupils were not affected in any way, positively or negatively, by factors relating to 'race' and background.

Of the nineteen pupils whom I thought were affected negatively, ten were similarly identified by teachers. But as discussed above, there were major differences between the set of factors identified by the teacher and myself and the weight we put on them. Of the other nine, two were thought to be affected positively, six not at all and in one case, the teacher did not give an answer.

Of the six pupils whom I thought were unaffected, four were similarly identified by teachers and two were thought by teachers to be positively affected.

Since the pupils' achievement may be reduced, it is surely important for teachers to reflect on the potentially negative experiences arising from children's encounters with racism or from differences between their home and the school environment. That teachers do not do this requires explanation.

One reason is that some teachers regard 'race' and background as very private areas. We saw how reluctant one teacher was to think about or 'intrude' into any child's background. Another, who was conscious of possible effects and even identified them, was nevertheless not keen to probe deeply and unwilling to discuss her observations with parents and worry them unduly. Among the three other teachers, this aspect of a pupil's achievement was simply something they had not thought about. Two said, on reflection, that they should have thought about it and that they would like to do so in the future.

135

Current Issues — Multicultural/Antiracist Education in the Classroom

I believe that multicultural education is good education and important for all children regardless of their background (see page 106) but, because this book focuses exclusively on pupils of Caribbean background, I am concentrating solely on the value of multicultural education to pupils of Caribbean heritage.

While none of the five teachers took account of 'race' and background effects in their analysis of individual pupil achievement, all argued that it is important for teachers in Britain to know about the cultural background of their pupils, and four of the five believed it important to have multicultural education in classrooms. This view is not universally held today.

An alternative view is that the key to academic success lies in schools that are managed well and good for all pupils. This view emphasises high achievement, a 'culture free' curriculum structured and effectively taught, and a pastoral care system that fosters children's confidence and motivation.

But will children of Caribbean heritage achieve fully in an educational system of this sort? Would they have equal opportunities? Almost surely not. The concept of a 'culture free' classroom is questionable. There are differences in culture. Children may be disadvantaged when the classroom does not reflect their home culture, for as the case studies show, this can lead to unacceptable behaviour, poor motivation, or a lack of confidence and security, all of which undermine achievement.

Strategies to maintain clear standards of behaviour and promote success in tasks may alleviate the problem but not remove it, since the underlying problem of cultural exclusion remains. With the dismissing of cultural differences, there is also a danger that teachers might unwittingly misinterpret situations and respond inappropriately, thus exacerbating the difficulties some pupils face. The conclusion, then, is that there cannot be equal opportunities for pupils of Caribbean heritage in a system perceived as 'good for all pupils, regardless of background', and staffed with teachers believing in the concept of a 'culture free' school.

A variation of the 'culture-free' school approach is that used by teachers who say that they 'treat all pupils the same'. These teachers maintain that opportunities are equal in their classes. The 'treat all pupils the same' philosophy has potentially different meanings and the consequences for equal opportunities depend on its interpretation.

At its most extreme and harmful, it may be used by racist teachers who do not wish to use a multicultural approach and are hostile or uncertain about pupils of Caribbean heritage. These teachers' philosophy of treating all children the same is unlikely to be reflected in their practice and their pupils will not have equal opportunities — this is explored further in the next chapter.

A second interpretation is offered by well-meaning teachers who genuinely believe in treating all children the same and, equally, think education can be culture-free. They will deliver a monocultural curriculum in a monocultural environment not reflecting the culture of pupils of Caribbean heritage, and thus disadvantaging them.

There are also teachers who recognise differences in culture even though they claim to 'treat all children the same'. Where such teachers empathise with children's lives, listen to and respond naturally and positively to aspects of culture different from their own, the consequences of a monocultural curriculum are less severe. This was true of one teacher in the study, and the evidence suggested that some children of Caribbean heritage succeed in classrooms of this sort. The situation is not ideal, however, since poor motivation, lack of confidence about identity, and problems over racism might undermine the achievement of others of Caribbean heritage.

What about teachers who believe in the value of a multicultural curriculum and try to reflect it in their practice, as did four of the teachers in the study? It seems to me that even such 'positive' classrooms may not be completely ideal.

In the study, the teachers' multicultural and in some cases antiracist philosophy was not reflected fully in practice. Inputs building on children's Caribbean backgrounds were occasional or done on a project basis, and did not generally take account of the reality of racism in Britain.

Children were not given the opportunities they needed to talk at length about Caribbean/ black British experiences. Moreover, even if this had been provided — through class-focused 'antiracist/ multicultural' practices — it might not have been enough to ensure the full achievement of all children of Caribbean heritage. There were differences between the pupils in their backgrounds, experiences and responses to 'race' and background encounters. Because of this, meeting the specific needs of any one child might require specific child-based approaches as well as whole-class strategies.

This raises some difficult and sensitive issues. Should there be greater openness and dialogue between a child's parents and teacher about any experiences arising from his/her 'race' and background? Should white teachers be actively involved in clarifying the effects of these on the child's progress, and in developing appropriate strategies for this child with the help and insight of the parents?

To give two examples, a child traumatised by racial harassment or a child acutely aware of racism in society, may suffer loss of confidence, in spite of the family having a very positive identity. The raising of these issues by parents with teachers who can empathise and reflect on these effects, just as they do about other underlying causes of lack of confidence, would increase the chance of developing remedies. Thus, the chances of ensuring equal opportunities is likely to be greater if teachers reflect on what 'race' and background influences are specific to a child, and their relevance, with the help of parents.

In short, I suggest that multicultural education is essential for equal opportunities. However, this approach as practised in some positive classrooms may not be sufficient to ensure full achievement by children of Caribbean heritage. Practice needs to reflect an 'anti-racist/multicultural' rather than a 'pure multicultural' philosophy, to be higher profile, consistent and to offer children opportunities for articulating and talking about racism. Moreover, strategies for the whole class may need to be accompanied by specific strategies focusing on individual children. Parents and teachers need to reflect on whether it is desirable to increase their dialogue about a child's background and experiences is desirable.

Black Pupils, 'Race' and Background

Looking at the way that children's experiences in the classroom are affected because they are black and of Caribbean background is not an easy task. Children's responses are complex and different, observations difficult to interpret, and great care is needed to ensure an open mind in the description and analysis of qualitative data. Also, the detail of a pupil's background and personal experiences constitutes a very sensitive and private area. For these reasons, some 'positive' teachers have been reluctant to venture deeply into this sphere.

Some children in the study were very centred in a Caribbean/black British culture. Others knew little and appeared to be seeking knowledge about their roots. A few suffered because home and classroom norms were different. Many were acquainted with racism, some to the extent of being aware of the nuances of differences in appearance and shades of colour. It seemed to me that a high profile 'anti-racist/multicultural' approach was needed to promote greater achievement, and also that teachers and parents might need to talk openly about a child's specific 'race' and background experiences.

Among the twenty-five pupils observed, some appeared not to be affected in any way by their being black and of Caribbean background. A few had positive experiences but this was of no relevance to their achievement. However for the majority of children in the case studies, experiences occurred which had a depressing effect on their achievement.

Some of the key variables through which achievement was affected were children's confidence, security, motivation and behaviour. A few interesting observations, tentative at this stage because of the small sample size, were made:

- A valuing of roots and confidence on the part of a young child is not sufficient to ensure that negative 'race' and background experiences do not occur.

- A family's valuing of roots, and the security of the child within it, sometimes contributes to confidence and achievement — but not in every case.

- Six/seven year old girls of Caribbean heritage do not have a greater chance of success than six/seven year old boys of Caribbean heritage.

It was noticeable that children's experiences were very different and their responses to situations varied considerably. Consequently it proved difficult to generalise about the specific nature of the processes through which confidence, security, motivation and behaviour were affected. Nevertheless, the outcomes were similar: for many pupils academic success was reduced.

Chapter 8

Racism, Racist Teachers, Pupil Experience

Chapter 2 looked briefly at five ethnographic studies of racism, all carried out after the publication of the Rampton Report (Department of Education and Science, 1981). It was suggested that life at school for pupils of Caribbean heritage was affected adversely by negative teacher attitudes.

Chapter 8 re-examines this conclusion in the light of a more critical examination of research published to date, incorporating twice as many studies as chapter 2, a more detailed and thorough description of individual studies, and an appraisal of methodology and of the difficulties inherent in researching a complex and potentially controversial area. This is essential for the evaluation of the research and the resulting conclusions and will be useful for practitioners interested in the nature and processes of racism in schools.

The chapter starts by defining racism and showing the reality of racism in action. After an intensive review of research, perceptions of racism in the nineteen nineties and their implications for racism in the future are considered.

Racism and Education — The Nineteen Eighties

While the term 'race' has little scientific validity, racism was and is very real in its existence and impact. In the nineteen eighties in Britain, it was common to define racism as 'prejudice plus power'. It was said that racist attitudes arose from a belief held by the majority white group that it was superior to minority groups, especially those of Caribbean, African and Asian origin, and that such attitudes were translated into practices that were likely to disadvantage minority groups.

In education, attention focused on clarifying the nature and dimensions of racism. Racism was said to operate at different levels. Most commonly, two levels were distinguished, the individual and the institutional (Department of Education and Science, 1981). But Figueroa's analysis, among others, distinguished cultural, individual, interpersonal, institutional and structural dimensions of racism (Figueroa, 1991).

It was recognised also that racism could be intentional or unintentional (Department of Education and Science, 1981). Even when unintentional, the effects of racism are harmful and so schools, local authorities and others interested in education put time and effort into learning and thinking about the different ways and levels at which racism operates. Amongst the advocates of multicultural education in the eighties were people who believed that the main cause of prejudice is ignorance, and that racist views can be dislodged by dialogue about beliefs and greater knowledge about other cultures and peoples (for criticism of this, see e.g. Troyna and Carrington, 1990).

A three level classification of racism (see opposite) sets the research described in this chapter in context. Examples are given for each level to illustrate the thinking and actions which may operate in the process of racism. The first, personal racism, deals with the more overt forms of racism evident in harassment and violence but it also includes aspects of interpersonal contact that may occur in racist encounters, such as ridicule, loaded language and the general disparaging and dismissing of ethnic minority experiences.

The second level is concerned with the stereotyping of the cultures of ethnic minorities. This form of racism, cultural racism, is particularly invidious. It is less overt and more difficult to handle, and can come from genuinely caring individuals as well as overt racists, with equally serious effects for ethnic minority pupils.

THE THREE FORMS OF RACISM *(Source: Shahid Ashrif, 1994)*

PERSONAL — Directed at Individuals:

- Racial harasment, violence. Attacks on black people or their property.
- Laughter, racist jokes, irrelevant references to origins, Disparaging backgrounds.
- Denying racism and identity ('I don't see their colour').
- Disrespect e.g. ignoring, or keeping waiting.
- Denial of personal experience of racism.
- Dismissing views of black people and their anger at racism experienced.
- Omitting to praise, reward, or to put in high profile situations not valuing contributions of black people.
- Excluding — e.g. from participation in certain activities; or from access to goods or services.

CULTURAL — statements and actions. Based on belief in white superiority, incorporated in stereotypes:

- Afro-Caribbeans (sic) are more musical, have natural rhythm, are naturally better athletes.
- Muggers are frequently Afro-Caribbean.
- Asian men are tyrannical, sexist.
- The Chinese are inscrutable, crafty.
- Afro-Caribbean pupils are disruptive, troublesome, innately low ability.
- Afro-Caribbean families are single parent families, hence all the problems.
- Asian pupils are hard working, deceitful.
- Britain civilized, helped the peoples of the empire. Latter in need of help, lacking in creativity, initiative, ability and capability to look after themselves.
- Catchphrase 'when in Rome...' which, it could be argued, is based on implicit understanding that such ways are superior, otherwise why copy them.
- Reduced/unbalanced opportunities arising from such beliefs on part of individual.
- Dismissing any cultural practices which are different as inferior or harmful.

INSTITUTIONAL — Long established practices and procedures which exclude ethnic minorities or reduce their access to opportunities or resources:

- Setting and disciplinary procedures which militate against black pupils.
- Curriculum which is eurocentric, fostering cultural racism.
- Poor guidance based on cultural stereotypes.
- Unnecessary rules which contravene basic cultural practices of minorities.
- Canteens or communications which exclude ethnic minority needs.
- All-white committees making decisions involving ethnic minority issues.
- Restricting black people to jobs which deal with black issues, marginalising them.
- Selection criteria for courses or jobs not related to the course or job, but based on English or on white European cultural norms.
- Current immigration laws in Britain.

Cultural racism includes situations where aspects of culture that differ from the white norm are automatically dismissed as inferior, and the many occasions when opportunities are reduced because of preconceived views about personalities, potential, or cultural norms.

The table gives examples of the sorts of stereotypes which exist. These may be difficult to dislodge. As one writer has said:

> We are not equally open to evidence on the characteristics of different people we meet; rather we are selectively cued to identify behaviour that fits our pre-conceived expectations .....A great deal of the power of the stereotype lies in the cumulative distortion that is generated through selective perception on the basis of characteristics identified as critical by stereotypes (Husband, 1986).

A third level of racism, one which was emphasised in antiracist teacher training in the eighties, is institutional racism. This is thought to arise from the combination of personal racism, cultural racism and of out-of-date rules leading to institutional practices and procedures which reduce equal opportunities for ethnic minorities. As the examples in the table illustrate, such practices and procedures cover many areas of school life. Among them are discriminatory grouping arrangements and a curriculum which is eurocentric.

As the author from whom the table was derived said, it is evident that racism 'like sexism, is a structural feature of society, and therefore a fundamental aspect of the way institutions function and consequently of the way groups and individuals interact'. What is not so evident — except to the targets of racism — is that not only is racism multifaceted, but it may be an everyday reality for black pupils, impinging on many areas of their life. Any single incident has to be seen in this context.

Published Research on Racism

Chapter two described five studies on racism, including research carried out after the publication of the Rampton Report (Department of Education and Science, 1981). This section will refer additionally to five studies carried out in the decade after Rampton. One was located in a single sex (boys) secondary school, a second examined both a single sex (boys) secondary school and a sixth form college (Foster, 1990. Mac an Ghail, 1988). Another focused solely on a sixth form college (Mac an Ghail,

1992). The last two, unusually, were located in primary schools (Wright, 1992. Tizard, 1988).

Particular attention will be paid to the conclusions of the ten studies concerning teacher attitudes, teacher-pupil interaction and the allocation of pupils to sets. The implications of the latter and the quality of advice on option and career choices for pupils of Caribbean heritage will be examined. Information about these ten studies is summarised on the following page, and set out in the order of the dates when the field work was done.

Excluding the study by Smith and Tomlinson and, for the moment, the research by Tizard et al, the earliest set of research in this decade included C, D, and E, all of which focused on pupils' experiences. While C and E looked at experiences generally but highlighted pupils' responses to the way they were perceived, D was particularly interested in career outcomes. As discussed below, all three consistently drew attention to teacher attitudes towards pupils of Caribbean heritage as a key problem.

1. Study C was located in two mixed comprehensives in the Midlands. Having spent 900 hours in the two schools, Wright's ethnographic approach led her to conclude that the pupils' experiences were strongly and negatively influenced by teachers' reactions to their 'race' and background. To illustrate the processes involved, she gave an account of an incident in one class and reported in full a discussion with a small group of pupils of Caribbean heritage. She did so for each of the two schools in the study.

One of the classroom accounts concerned a heated and angry confrontation about jokes and racism between a teacher and black pupils. This arose when the teacher, aggravated by the rising level of noise in the class, threw a piece of chalk at a pupil of Caribbean heritage who, according to the researcher, was not 'being particularly noisy'. The account of the confrontation and talk with the researcher indicated that this teacher was overtly racist and known for making disparaging comments and jokes about pupils' colour and background. In this school the small group discussion, reported by the researcher and involving eight boys of Caribbean heritage, was dominated by pupils quoting the teacher's racist remarks and their anger about it. In the discussion, four other teachers were described as prejudiced.

	Date of Field Work	Size of study	Age Location	Author	Date Published
	TEN STUDIES — RESEARCH ON RACISM 1980s AND EARLY 1990s				
A	Longitudinal study 81/82, 82/83, 83/84, 84/85, 85/86	Large scale 20 schools 3000 pupils	11/12 in 81/82 4 areas	Smith and Tomlinson	1989
B	Logitudinal study 82/83, 83/84, 84/85	Small scale 30+schools 4 pupils in each	5/6 in 82/83 London	Tizard, Blatchford, Burke, Farquhar, Plewis	1988
C	1982-1984	Small scale 2 schools Fourth Form, Fifth Form	14/15, 15/16 Midlands Comp.	Wright	1985
D	Early eighties 18 month period	Small scale 2 schools 62 in Fifth and Sixth Form; 27 in Third	15/16 to 18/19; 13/14 1 single sex	Mirza	1992
E	a) 1980-1982 b) 1983-1985	Small scale 1 school 1 Sixth Form College	Single Sex	Mac an Ghail	1988
F	1984/1986	Small scale 1 school	13/14 Midlands Inner City Comp.	Gillborn	1990
G	1985/1986	Small scale 1 school	13/14 to 15/16 Inner City Comp.	Foster	1990
H	1986-1988	Small scale 1 college	17/18, 18/19 Mixed Sixth Form College	Mac an Ghail	1992
I	1987-1989	Small scale 4 schools	Primary (3-8), Middle	Wright	1992
J	1990	Small scale	11/12	Brook	1991

The classroom incident in the second school also illustrated the consequences of unfair treatment by a teacher. In this case a teacher unfairly reprimanded a group of girls of Caribbean heritage. The girls responded angrily and a teacher-pupil confrontation developed. Comments made by the teacher in the informal discussion with the researcher afterwards suggested that the teacher saw the girls as a threat, expected trouble from them, and generally perceived them as unpredictable and potentially resentful and confrontational.

In the discussion with five girls of Caribbean heritage in this school, the current Head, the previous Head, the Deputy and five other teachers were said to be prejudiced. The girls described a variety of examples of unfair treatment, and also teacher statements not dissimilar to those in the other school e.g. about going back to 'your own country', being called monkey, and also a case of a pupil's friend being told that 'she is only getting bad because she hangs around with too many black people'.

In both schools, there were examples of unacceptable pupil behaviour. In one case, a pupil of Caribbean heritage threw a book at a teacher after the teacher had thrown it at the pupil. In another case, a pupil pushed a teacher after she had been pushed by the teacher. Pupils of Caribbean heritage clearly challenged teachers, not only by treatment mirroring that which a teacher had just meted out, but also by swearing and using unacceptable language. Thus, even if the pupils perceived their actions as a response to teachers' lack of respect for their backgrounds, their own behaviour could be described as poor and unacceptable. Sometimes pupils used dialect because they knew that this threatened and angered teachers.

From incidents of unfair treatment such as the two described, and from discussions with teachers and pupils, Wright argued that it was teacher attitudes that led to confrontations and to the poor pupil behaviour and so were the major problem.

An examination of the sets in which pupils worked showed that pupils of Caribbean heritage were less well represented in higher ability sets. Wright argued that this was the result of teacher attitudes, which had a direct effect on pupil allocation to groups. They also had an additional and indirect effect because teachers were reluctant to have pupils perceived as trouble-makers in certain teaching groups. Wright thus demonstrated that teacher attitudes played a key role in reducing access for pupils of Caribbean heritage to academic opportunities.

2. Study D differentiated between teachers. One third of the fifty teachers in the two schools involved were described as 'overt racists' and a quarter were said to be 'liberal chauvinists'. The remainder, apart from a 'black teacher' and a 'crusader', were described as 'christians'.

Mirza visited two schools over a period of eighteen months, spending time with teachers in staff rooms, with pupils and teachers in classrooms, and interviewing small and large groups of pupils. Teachers classified by her as 'overt racists' were those who used terms such as 'wog' or who, in conversations with pupils, made irrelevant and 'putting down' references to their background e.g. semi-facetious remarks about peanuts or coconuts. These teachers regarded pupils of Caribbean heritage as 'loud and inconsiderate'.

In some cases, parents of Caribbean heritage, too, received less good treatment e.g. by being being made to wait unduly to see teachers. There were examples also of preconceived notions about what black people are capable of, for instance teachers being amazed when they saw that the Local Education Authority Officer who arrived to visit the school was black.

The 'liberal chauvinists' believed that they knew and understood black families and culture. Nevertheless their actions had racist undertones and their comments, according to Mirza, illustrated that parents of Caribbean heritage were perceived as less good. Her chapter, 'Life in the Classroom', gave specific examples illustrating teacher perception of parents as educationally backward and having cultural practices that disadvantaged their children. Some parents were viewed as having completely unrealistic expectations for their children, teacher perceptions which the researcher judged incorrect from her in-depth knowledge of the pupils and parents concerned.

Apart from one black teacher and one 'crusader', the remaining teachers were described as 'christians'. These were teachers who talked about not 'seeing any difference' and not perceiving 'problems'. Nevertheless, some 'christians' patronised pupils and families of Caribbean heritage, treating them differently to white pupils, in spite of not 'seeing any difference'.

Although Mirza did not explicitly consider behaviour, it would appear from her book that pupils were motivated and worked and behaved reasonably well. There was some unacceptable behaviour in the form of 'messing about' in lessons, but mostly so in the lessons perceived by pupils as less useful for their academic and career outcomes.

Negative teacher attitudes affected the pupils' experiences and outcomes. Coming from a culture which values education, the sixty-two girls of Caribbean heritage in Mirza's study had a positive attitude to education and a desire and commitment to maximising their academic attainment. In spite of this, their subject choices and academic opportunities were restricted because the girls adopted strategies to avoid problems, problem teachers and situations they thought likely to provoke them into challenging the teachers' racist assumptions.

Moreover, their choice of subjects and career possibilities were limited by the poor career advice available to all pupils, and by teacher stereotyping and stereotypical advice which meant that they lost out even more. Setting and streaming at an early stage in the school, in which low teacher expectations played a role, also restricted their academic opportunities and, therefore, their later career choices.

Thus, although the processes differ in detail from those described by Wright, teacher attitudes again contributed to pupils' disadvantage, as in Wright's study.

3. Study E was based on a period of two years during which Mac an Ghail spent time with specific groups of boys in a single sex school and with their teachers. The teachers generally had little contact with and knew little about the ethnic minority communities from which their students came.

Like Mirza's study, study E distinguished between teachers. Of the thirty-three full-time and the three part-time teachers, Mac an Ghail perceived seventeen as being 'overt racists' and five as 'new realists'. Ten were seen as 'liberals', more aware of ethnic minority needs and interested in developing the curriculum appropriately to reflect backgrounds. Their efforts in this direction were thwarted by non-cooperative students.

The 'liberals' were forced to operate within the racist context of the school. Racist stereotyping was illustrated by Mac an Ghail in incidents and statements showing the tendency for pupils of Caribbean heritage to be seen as difficult and troublesome. He also noted racist stereotypical assumptions not restricted to the school and education, such as associating West Indians with the mugging of old ladies.

According to Mac an Ghail, this system of racist stereotyping affected grouping procedures. Placement at entry, third year option decisions, and exam preparation in the fifth form all ensured that pupils of Caribbean heritage had less access to the better resources and teaching available to the higher achieving sets.

The racism inherent in teacher attitudes, sometimes overtly expressed, affected the way that pupils were treated. Pupils of Caribbean heritage were divided by Mac an Ghail into 'Soul Heads', 'Funk Heads', and 'Rasta Heads', and the book concentrated on the latter.

Mac an Ghail's analysis stressed the Rasta Heads' effectiveness in promoting success on their own terms. Work was not a priority and they were predominantly academic underachievers. Their success came from the high profile and value placed by the group on appearing to be strong and able to assert themselves, and from the admiration this drew from their peers at school. Their strategy in managing their experience of racism was to 'invert the dominant ideology', to reject schooling actively and visibly in a number of ways e.g. arriving late, creating disturbances by demanding seats, sucking their teeth and using bad looks, refusing 'to be shamed' and acting tough.

The pupils saw these encounters differently from teachers. The boys' perceptions, articulated by Mac an Ghail, were of experiences of teacher racism. The consequence was a strategy of overtly negative and confrontational approaches to school and teachers. For their part, the teachers saw the 'Rasta Heads' as disciplinary problems, uncooperative and having a bad effect on the rest of the school.

A follow-up study by Mac an Ghail also used a very open-ended ethnographic and participative approach, but this time he analysed a group from a sixth form college and focused on ethnic minority girls. Quotations from these girls, whom he called the 'Black Sisters', indicated that racism was part of their educational experience. As with the boys in the single sex school, pupil-teacher interactions were characterised by teacher stereotyping of Caribbean students as having lower ability and being troublesome. A monocultural curriculum and poor advice, arising from teachers' perceptions that pupils had exaggerated expectations of their abilities, were also evident.

The behaviour of these girls was not ideal. They were achievers and their positive attitudes were reflected in many ways: good attendance, hard work and completion of homework. This was part of a strategy of 'resistance within accommodation' for, although the girls were not overtly confrontational, they demonstrated their feelings about the unequal treatment received by deliberate incidents such as being late, handing in homework late, and not participating in group discussions.

Mac an Ghail also described his analysis of the experiences of a group of 'Asian Warriors' in the single sex school referred to above. His overall conclusions was that the 'Rasta Heads', the 'Black Sisters' and the 'Asian Warriors' all experienced a different reality from white pupils, that all three groups identified racism as the major problem in their schooling and that, in their different ways, they evolved strategies of resistance to racism which cut across gender divisions.

4. Study F: The next two studies to be discussed were carried out in the mid-eighties. In study F, Gillborn extended and developed the thesis that teacher approaches to pupils of Caribbean heritage were the key to black pupils' poor behaviour.

In the course of his visits, three or more times a week to a boys school over three terms, he came to the conclusion that pupils of Caribbean heritage were more criticised and controlled. This was based on many hours observing lessons and records made of critical and controlling statements.

Additional evidence that black pupils were more likely to be thought by teachers to cause concern came from Gillborn's analysis of report cards received by pupils during their school career. Being given a card indicated that there was problem behaviour which warranted formal structured monitoring by all teachers in contact with the pupil. Gillborn found that boys of Caribbean heritage were disproportionately represented amongst those who received at least one card. There was further evidence in the records of detentions which showed that boys of Caribbean heritage were more likely to receive punishment for vague reasons and were disproportionately represented amongst those given at least one detention during seven terms.

Gillborn's development of the argument that pupils of Caribbean heritage were being singled out for criticism, i.e that they received unequal and unfair treatment and were in effect 'picked on', had several strands. One was the evidence from his observations and statements from pupils.

Gillborn argued that his own observations suggested undue criticism and he illustrated this with an account of one incident.

This evidence was complemented and confirmed by the perceptions of pupils from a variety of backgrounds. That it was generally thought that pupils of Caribbean heritage were unduly criticised was evident in Gillborn's extracts from conversations with black pupils, and in white pupils' answers to questions such as 'Do you think the teachers particularly like or dislike some people?', 'Do you think that any groups of pupils are treated differently?', 'Do the teachers treat any groups of pupils differently?'

A second strand in Gillborn's argument came from discussions with teachers. These indicated that some teachers tended to stereotype pupils, and to make generalisations about problem behaviour on the part of black pupils. He illustrated this by quoting one teacher's comments to him.

A third and quite powerful strand was the analysis of the way that pupils of Caribbean heritage reacted to their experiences in the classroom. Gillborn observed that pupil behaviour ranged from 'resistance and confrontation' through to 'accommodation', and cited discussions with pupils as evidence of the two extreme types. He described 'resistance', quoting from two pupils in this category. 'Accommodation' was illustrated by quoting from one pupil and by additional evidence from a conversation with a white pupil who was highly committed to school.

Gillborn's argument was that, in spite of the range of pupil behaviour, incidents of undue criticism of pupils occurred across the response range, thus suggesting that the difference in criticism and control by teachers was due not to differences in behaviour but to differences in teacher perceptions of black pupils.

Gillborn's conclusions differed from those of others in earlier studies in his identification of a wide variety of pupil responses and his finding that boys whose behaviour was characterised by 'resistance' were not necessarily alienated from the culture of school. But his main conclusion, that teacher perceptions were a key and causal factor, was similar to that of earlier researchers. This was not the case with study G .

5. Study G: Foster located his research in a boys' school, created in an inner city in 1967. The school had a history of interest in multicultural education and equal opportunities, establishing a policy on multicultural education in May 1980, and among the first schools in Britain to do so.

Foster used a systematic approach to examine the effect of teacher attitudes in this context. The current logic appeared to be:

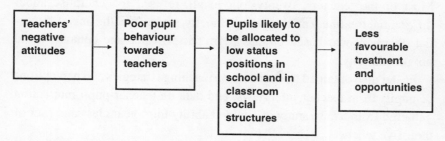

Accordingly, Foster aimed to see whether these stages were in operation in the school and also whether staff in a school committed to equal opportunities had succeeded in creating a non-racist environment. His field work was carried out in the academic year 1985/1986, when he spent three days each week in the school.

Like other researchers, Foster employed ethnographic techniques. His informal observations revealed few expressed racist attitudes on the part of staff and no over-representation of students of Caribbean heritage in disciplinary incidents. Conflict between teachers and pupils, of the sort observed by Wright, did not occur nor were there adverse teacher responses to dialect or misunderstandings by teachers of pupils' non-verbal communication.

Interviews with thirty-one fifth year pupils, chosen to include a mixture of pro-school and anti-school pupils, and small group discussions with twenty-two fourth years, showed that pupils generally perceived teacher racism as a relatively limited phenomenon in their school. Examples of incidents tended to be restricted to a teacher who was no longer at the school. Only three pupils complained, without being asked, about what they felt was racism from their teachers. One who 'had been in a lot of trouble in school and felt that he was picked on', and the other two, 'when pressed ...found it difficult to specify exactly what they meant and to give examples of incidents which they felt showed 'prejudice''.

Foster supplemented these data with other systematic investigations. He carried out formal interviews with thirty-two teachers using two open-ended questions, one asking what teachers felt were the main characteristics of different ethnic groups, and the second focusing on whether teachers adjusted their approach to suit different ethnic groups.

There were two teachers with negative and stereotypical views, and six who generalised about groups of students but did so 'very tentatively'. Most of the teachers, twenty-four in all, refused to generalise about differential treatment arising from ethnicity, saying that the only differential treatment was based on classroom performance and behaviour and not on ethnicity.

Foster also obtained information on teaching strategies and perceptions of pupils from teacher interviews, and data on teacher-pupil interaction gathered from a case study of a mixed ability third year class and four of their five teachers.

The conclusion from the complete set of teacher interviews and the third year case study tended to confirm the picture that the environment was generally free of racism. Foster's conclusion that staff treated pupils equally and that differences, where they occurred, were attributable to pupils' ability and behaviour, was therefore very different to that of other researchers.

Nevertheless, Foster's data on settings for different curricular areas suggested that boys, and especially Afro-Caribbean boys, were more likely to be in lower status groups and to be under-represented in higher status groups. This was most noticeable in English, where only four per cent of boys of Caribbean heritage in the fourth year were in the top set even though they accounted for twenty-eight per cent of the 103 students in the year.

Their lesser representation in higher status groups appeared to be for behavioural reasons, with the teachers looking at past behaviour and output as indicators of motivation. Behaviour was frequently used as a criterion in allocating pupils to sets, in addition to pupil ability as indicated by performance.

Foster argued that motivation is a valid criterion in such decisions as it indicates 'which students are likely to make best use of a place in a high status group' and helps to determine 'the optimum make-up of classes ..... in order to maximise the achievement of all students'. According to Foster, it is not valid for researchers such as Wright to critise teachers for using behavioural criteria in allocating pupils to sets. Thus, while highlighting pupil behaviour as an important element in preventing access to achievement, this researcher's view was that negative teacher attitudes did not contribute to pupils' disadvantage.

The last three studies listed on page 146, are based on field work carried out in the late nineteen eighties and published in the early nineteen nineties. Two of them, studies H and I, by researchers who published in the earlier phase of research, agree with earlier studies that negative teacher attitudes are an important barrier to equal opportunities. As will be seen, racism appears to be less overt than in earlier years but stereotyping and unequal treatment continue to be part of the school experiences of pupils of Caribbean heritage.

6. Study H, by Mac an Ghail, explored the perceptions of pupils at a sixth form college. One student referred to the stereotyping by teachers of pupils of Caribbean heritage as being good at sport. Another said that teachers did not encourage black pupils to do the 'good' subjects but channelled them towards sport and music. Students thought that teachers saw students of Caribbean heritage as difficult and poorly behaved and, according to one student of Caribbean heritage, 'while Asians were seen as good, we were seen as bad'.

The extent of the repercussions of having racist teachers, and the degree of disadvantage suffered, depended on the student's responses to racism. As with the 'accommodating' boys in Gillborn's study and the girls in Mirza's study, some of these higher-achieving students were aware of the need to take steps to avoid problems arising from racist teacher attitudes. One referred to the trouble caused by challenging teachers, another to the fact that a student might be worse off if he/she fought racism. A student talked about incidents of teacher racism directed at pupils not working as they should, saying about the teacher racism: 'Of course that was still wrong but it seemed to me that if you worked then you got on OK. .. .. I think that if you see the racism clearly at this stage, then it's more difficult to get through or at least if you openly fight it, then it is.' Another talked about deliberately cultivating the teachers 'with whom one gets on'.

Some pupils were less willing to compromise. One said 'One day I came into class and my hair was in plaits. This teacher said, you look like a troublemaker. He was obviously racist. He thought a high achiever wouldn't identify with what is black. You are supposed to act white, if you want to survive here. Well, I stayed black and got through without their help.'

7. Study I, by Wright, was based on research done between 1987 and 1989, located in three schools for five to eight year olds and in the middle school to which all the pupils transferred. The method used was primarily ethnographic but notes from observations during the time spent in a school were supplemented by school records on withdrawal of pupils from their classroom for 'an alleged 'deviant act'', and by records of the teachers' confidential comments on the pupils' transfer documents.

The researcher's first impression of teachers was that they were genuinely pleasant, constructive and caring about the pupils. But observations over time led her to the conclusion that pupils of ethnic minority origin were seen by teachers as causing classroom management problems and treated differently from the white pupils.

Wright illustrated the difference in treatment between pupils of Caribbean heritage and white pupils by describing two incidents in a school. One involved a very young pupil, a four year old who was perceived by the teacher as 'boisterous, verging on disruptive'. To the researcher, the child appeared bright and enthusiastic, eager to participate in the group discussion. His desire to contribute was constantly ignored. Keen to answer the teacher's question, the child called out the correct answer. The teacher responded by telling the child, crossly, not to shout out. Other children who called out but were white were not reprimanded in this way. The other incident involved an eight year old who was shown in the researcher's account of the incident to be singled out unfairly for criticism and exclusion.

Wright quoted discussions with black carers in two of the schools, who clearly felt that staff did not take the same care in settling down children of Caribbean heritage as they did for white pupils, and that the needs of black pupils were not being accommodated. Conversations with pupils of Caribbean heritage, from the third of the first schools and from the middle school, revealed that they thought that black pupils were generally 'picked on' and not always treated equally when responsibilities and rewards were allocated. That pupils of Caribbean heritage were unfairly picked on by teachers was confirmed also in conversations with white pupils at the middle school.

The researcher noted that physical restraint was more commonly used with pupils of Caribbean heritage and reported conversations with two teachers and one headteacher that confirmed this. One teacher saw this method as 'the only way of controlling children who were full of aggression'.

Examination of school records on withdrawal for one term, confirmed that children of Caribbean heritage did experience greater control in the form of disciplinary action. In one of the first schools, six of the seventy-nine pupils of Caribbean heritage were withdrawn compared with two of the 131 white pupils. In another first school, seven of the fifty-four pupils of Caribbean heritage were withdrawn at some stage during the term, but only two of the seventy-nine white pupils. In the middle school, two of the thirty-seven pupils of Caribbean heritage were thus sanctioned in contrast to only one of the 111 white pupils. Withdrawals generally involved boys but in one of the first schools, two of the children of Caribbean heritage withdrawn were girls.

The researcher also presented teachers' confidential comments on the pupils transferring from one of the schools. According to her analysis, although positive comments were made about pupils of Caribbean heritage and they obtained high gradings for ability, a disproportionate number were presented as having behavioural problems and fewer positive comments were made about them than about other groups of children.

Wright concluded that although teachers perceived pupils of Caribbean heritage as management problems and treated them differently, they were not overtly racist or hostile to pupils, nor were they completely unaware or unwilling to consider the children's needs. Some made efforts to bring multiculturalism into the classroom. Positive images were evident in the schools, books with a multicultural theme in one school, displays including black children and adults in a variety of roles in another, and positive books and displays in another. In the Middle School, a multicultural theme was apparent in the teaching materials.

Nevertheless, differences in treatment were evident in the teachers' interactions with pupils and their application of control and sanctions, which the researcher explained by the difference in the way that teachers perceived the pupils.

Interviews with a sample of the parents showed that parents of Caribbean heritage were concerned about race relations and felt that their children experienced racial prejudice from teachers. They were also dissatisfied with school activities and the standard of work at school.

8. Study A by Smith and Tomlinson, like Study B by Tizard et al, was a longitudinal study, started in the early eighties. Both were very different from the work in later years. In neither case was there any attempt to examine teachers' attitudes in depth or to use ethnographic techniques for examining pupils' experiences.

Smith and Tomlinson followed a group of children, from their transfer to secondary schools in 1981 at the age of eleven, through to the fifth form. Tizard et al followed children from the age of five in 1982 through the next two years of infant school.

Study A was considered in chapter 2. A major objective was to research differences between schools and their effectiveness. Smith and Tomlinson obtained no good comprehensive data from teacher questionnaires, because some teachers were reluctant to cooperate with the study. Among the many reasons given for this lack of cooperation was the association of the research with racial and ethnic minority groups, a connection which the authors said was likely to make teachers defensive and sensitive lest they be accused of racism. Ethnic minority families comprised 42 per cent of the study families, one-sixth of them originating from the Caribbean.

Any evidence on teacher attitudes had to be obtained from the survey of parents or from pupil questionnaires, neither of which asked direct questions about teacher attitudes or racism. The parent survey asked about contacts with school, and about satisfaction or dissatisfaction with schools. Parents rarely mentioned racism in their responses. Of the 2075, one per cent mentioned racial attacks or other matters such as their dissatisfaction because black children and white did not get on. Only eight parents said that teachers were prejudiced. Thus the authors concluded that their findings gave little support for reports such as the Burnage High School Inquiry which, according to Smith and Tomlinson, had 'created the impression that overt racism is a serious problem in multi-ethnic schools'.

The pupil questionnaire focused on children's feelings about school, about the praise and blame they received from heads and teachers, about participation in activities and friendship patterns, and about attendance. The aspect most relevant to the current chapter concerns the praise and blame received. It was found that ethnic minority pupils received 'a bit more praise than children originating from the UK'. It was also noted, although not commented on at any length, that 'children of West Indian origin receive distinctly more criticism than those originating in the UK, who in turn receive more than children of South Asian origin'.

Other data collected included behavioural scores from the feeder primary schools. Again, results are consistent with other research. It was found that children of West Indian origin were more likely than white pupils to have exhibited behavioural problems.

9. Study B, by Tizard et al, was on a much smaller scale than Smith and Tomlinson's. It was located in thirty schools in London and sampled four children in each school, one boy and girl of Caribbean heritage, and one white boy and girl. The study examined the effect of school on achievement and the contribution made by homes in the development of young children. It was interested in differences in achievement and its causes.

Field work in classrooms used a systematic observation of classroom learning time to examine the curriculum on offer to different pupils. No differences were found in the curriculum received by different ethnic groups. As with many of the other studies, this study also revealed differences in pupil-teacher interaction and pupil behaviour. Observations indicated that black boys had less work contacts with teachers and received the most criticism and disapproval. Black boys were observed to 'mess around more', and interviews with both pupils and teachers suggested that their behaviour was not as good as white children's. Poor behaviour did not appear to be restricted to the boys. Black girls, too, said that they got into trouble for being naughty and teacher interviews suggested that they had at least as many behavioural problems as black boys and more than white girls. Although this study examined teacher attitudes, it was primarily in regard to their expectations of pupils and their views about adopting a multicultural curriculum.

Teacher racism was not examined as such but a comparison was made of teacher expectations with pupil achievement. There was no evidence of low teacher expectations for black children overall. In Maths, there appeared to be a tendency towards high expectations of black boys and low expectations of white girls. The researchers explained the high expectations for black boys by saying that teachers expected boys to be better at maths and that they over-emphasised the potential achievement of black boys because they did not want to appear biased against black pupils. Attitudes to multicultural education were also examined, primarily with respect to the school as a whole, and a multicultural score was allocated to each school.

Name-calling was investigated through pupil interviews. This showed that children were called a variety of names and black pupils suffered from racist taunts.

10. Study J: Finally, it is useful to look at the research by Brook, already referred to in chapter 2. The study is particularly interesting in view of the consistent theme of differences in teachers' treatment of different groups of pupils. Brook's systematic and statistical analysis of teacher-pupil interactions confirmed that pupils of Caribbean heritage received significantly more negative comments than other pupils. The researcher found that the teachers he interviewed tended to have a limited awareness of pupils' cultural and social backgrounds and negative perceptions of them. Pupil interviews tended to single out one particular teacher as racist.

Some of the difficulties of doing research on racism are now considered and I will try to clarify what conclusions can be drawn from the body of research as a whole.

Racist Encounters at the Individual Level

The Swann Report considered the research on teacher stereotyping, teacher expectations, and school performance and concluded:

> While we do not retreat from our earlier conclusions about the influence of teachers (i.e. those in the Interim Report stressing the importance of racism) we do think that the problem is complex and subtle and needs much more research if it is ever to be understood in full (Department of Education and Science, 1985).

The Report did not expand on what they meant by the 'complexity' and the 'subtlety' of the problem. One issue is to do with the intricacies of 'racist' encounters between people from the white majority population and people from ethnic minority groups. As we saw from the examples in the first section of this chapter and the ethnographic studies, these are many and varied.

The research illustrated that interactions might use verbal cues with overtly racist language or irrelevant references about background to convey hostility, derision, disparagement, exclusion or racist stereotyping. It is equally possible that communication imbued with underlying racist attitudes and conveying negative feelings is expressed verbally, but without any clear evidence of a link with the background of the recipient. Communication of racist attitudes through body language and non-verbal cues can complicate racist interactions still further. The recipient may pick up the messages of racism but find it difficult to say why they perceived the interaction as racist. The reader may have noticed some of these complexities in the examples described in this book.

The impact of racism on a child or an adult can be intense. Racism, at its various levels, may be a consistent and ongoing reality of everyday life for the recipient, with its multiplicity of experiences — denying, disparaging, dismissing, abusing, excluding. The injustice and unfairness, the pain and damage is accentuated because of this context and felt even more powerfully because similar experiences may be hurting others in the group with which the recipient identifies, including their nearest and dearest — their parents and children.

Not surprisingly, recipients develop skills to help them to interpret interactions and, some would argue, can frequently identify the encounters that are racist. The incident itself may provide evidence of this. The context of the interaction may furnish additional clues. Other racist incidents with the person concerned, experienced either by the recipient or by trusted peers, friends and family, may influence the way the incident is interpreted. Because of the subtlety and complexity of racism and the processes of interpretation, recipients may 'pick up the vibes' of racism, but if asked to describe exactly what happened and why the interaction was racist, find it difficult to produce firm evidence.

While intense emotions may be aroused on the part of the recipient, those said to be racist can also experience strong feelings. Some may have overt and hostile racist attitudes, others may be unintentionally racist. People accused of racism can become defensive, as is clear in some of the incidents described by Wright. Feelings of embarrassment, humour, fear or uncertainty are all common reactions and the valid feelings of the recipients are dismissed, and the existence of racism denied.

Nor are individuals always consistent. Some people may act in a racist way in one situation and a non-racist way in another. As one researcher said in a life history of a senior teacher at a school: 'ambiguities, inconsistencies and ambivalences... can arise amongst those with racist attitudes' (Bagley, 1992).

All individuals differ and some white people do not have racist attitudes towards people of Caribbean heritage. The person accused of racism in a specific incident might not have racist attitudes but be misunderstood or associated with people who are racist. It seems likely that, when accused of racism, such people would experience feelings of defensiveness. And because it may be difficult for those with no personal experience of racism to understand the impact and potential intensity of the experience on a recipient, the reactions of recipients may seem strange. Non-racists and racists might both claim that 'X' has a 'chip on the shoulder'.

In short, interactions which are racist or perceived as such, are fraught and likely to precipitate intense feelings on the part of all involved. Differences in the personal experience and backgrounds of the parties involved may influence perspectives and the way each perceives the interaction.

Evaluating Research on Racism

There have been differences in opinion about the validity of some of the research on racism in the classroom (Foster, 1990b. Connoly, 1992). This is not surprising in what is a complex, emotionally-loaded and potentially controversial research field. This section examines the strengths of published studies, but offers first some caveats about the evaluation of qualitative studies.

Qualitative research can be structured or unstructured. A qualitative study which incorporates the traditional ethnographic approach is unstructured and the researcher is expected to participate and empathise with the experiences of those who are the focus of the study, discerning patterns through their continuing and complete immersion in detailed transcripts (Edwards and Furlong, 1985). Because of the potential for differing perspectives, the researcher's conclusions may be criticised by others who 'feel' that their observation is invalid and argue that the processes have been misinterpreted.

In a qualitative approach, very detailed evidence may be collected but the scope of the study may be limited. This could lead to problems where there are differences in perspective. Critics might argue, sometimes unjustifiably, that only a partial picture of an incident has been presented, that important other factors have been omitted, that incidents have been taken out of context, the dynamics of the situation omitted, or an incorrect impression of key causal factors given.

Difficulties abound in using the qualitative approach. Some are due to the great care researchers have to take to ensure that their conclusions are not influenced by their own perspective. Problems can occur in the design of the study, in its implementation and the validation of data collected, or in the analysis and the presentation of the study to readers. The author has been reflecting on and developing criteria to improve effectiveness in each of these four areas. It is not appropriate to detail these in this book, but a few of the potential difficulties are indicated.

Looking first at design, implementation and analysis, it is essential for researchers to specify their sampling unit. It is not clear from reading some reports how widely this has been done, or even whether the sampling unit has been identified. Where the parameters are set out, the collection of data within the unit may not include a representative selection of sources or a wide enough range of data for patterns observed to be properly validated. Another problem is that researchers may generalise, unjustifiably, from the sampling unit to others not included properly in the project.

The analysis and presentation of results can also be problematic. With the detailed and often unstructured qualitative information collected, identifying patterns and then selecting illustrations for them is time-consuming, and requires great care to ensure that the evidence collected is adequate and the presentation is clear to readers.

Let us move on to specific qualitative studies, focusing on those whose conclusions are consistent with a theory of teacher racism as a cause of unequal treatment and identifying the focus and strengths of each. These include Studies C, D, E, F, H, and also I, since although teachers were said not to be overtly racist or hostile in this study, they treated black children and white differently. Study C, by Wright, centred on pupil experiences, through classroom observations over 900 hours in two schools. It succeeded in giving a graphic and convincing description, including one incident in each of two classrooms, illustrating the patterns observed in the process of interaction between pupils and teachers (Wright, 1985).

The study by Mirza incorporated the whole school in the sampling unit, with all the complexity which exists in a secondary school, so a wider range of processes were covered. This was useful in enabling the study to throw light on the multiplicity of possible effects of racism, identified in the first section of this chapter. It was also able to highlight the differences between teachers' attitudes but their implications for structures within the school and for the experiences of individual pupils was not examined in any depth (Mirza, 1992).

Mac an Ghail's was an ethnographic study, with a convincing presentation of students' experiences. Unlike Wright, he was in constant contact with specified groups of pupils and his approach was primarily participatory. He used conversations with students as evidence of their perceptions of their experiences, and as a basis for analysis of their responses (Mac an Ghail, 1988). The other study by Mac an Ghail, also described above, employed a similar approach (Mac an Ghail, 1992).

Gillborn's work used a year group in a secondary school as a sampling unit, and concentrated on teacher actions rather than teacher attitudes. It avoided some of the potential criticisms in this controversial area by focusing on action and using the technique of 'triangulation' i.e. including additional and independent sources of data to test his own observations of patterns (Gillborn, 1990).

Wright's more recent study included powerfully convincing descriptions of episodes, said by her to illustrate the patterns she observed. This later study had the additional advantage of including objective and independent data supporting some of her observations (Wright, 1992).

Although each study has strengths, especially when evaluated in terms of its own focus and objectives, careful scrutinising in light of my list of criteria suggests that each can be faulted on several grounds. This makes it difficult to draw firm conclusions from any one study. Rather than expanding on individual 'defects', the need for developing agreed criteria for future research is emphasised, and the discussion moves on to seeing what conclusions can be derived from the research as a whole.

Can Conclusions be Drawn?

Overall, the ten studies described show that white teachers may have certain views about pupils of Caribbean background. Some teachers think that these pupils are disruptive and a management problem (Wright, 1985, 1992. Mac an Ghail, 1988, 1992). Some believe that they will achieve less than white children, and that their parents are not as capable as white parents (Mirza, 1992). Some teachers are hostile to pupils of Caribbean background and combine overt racism with jokes about backgrounds, as shown in some of the earlier studies (Wright, 1988).

According to black pupils and white and, in some studies also peripatetic teachers, pupils of Caribbean heritage may be 'picked on' (Gillborn, 1990. Wright, 1985. Wright, 1992). Frequently, teachers are shown to be critical and on occasions to 'put students down'. They address more negative comments to pupils of Caribbean heritage, exercise more control over them and, at a primary level, may not give the positive pastoral care needed for young children (Wright, 1985, 1992. Mac an Ghail, 1988, 1992. Gillborn, 1990. Smith and Tomlinson, 1989. Tizard et al,1988. Brook, 1991).

Pupils of Caribbean heritage may be placed in lower status groups by teachers and hence unduly represented in such sets (Wright, 1985. Mirza, 1992. Mac an Ghail, 1988. Foster, 1990). Pupils may themselves go for less favourable options if this helps them avoid problems with racist teachers (Mirza, 1992).

Much of the debate about what can be concluded from research has revolved around the question: 'are teachers racist and is this the cause of the observed difference in treatment of and the unequal opportunities offered to pupils of Caribbean heritage?' One proponent of the view that we have insufficient evidence to answer this key question in the affirmative targeted the study published by Wright in 1985 for criticism (Foster, 1990).

This pioneering work by Wright had sought to look at pupils' experiences and identify and elucidate the processes underlying them. Foster questioned the validity and representativeness of the evidence she described, apparently missing the point of Wright's study and completely dismissing the perceptions by the black pupils of their own experiences. Other criticisms made by Foster are more fundamental and deserve closer scrutiny.

Foster argued that the key to the treatment of pupils of Caribbean heritage — hostility and a relatively greater degree of control and punishment — lay in their own poor behaviour. He suggested an alternative explanation, arguing that the cycle of hostile teacher-pupil relations started with poor behaviour by pupils, due not to negative teacher attitudes but to the pupils' anti-school attitudes. These, he suggested, might arise from:

outside the school in the social structural situation of Afro- Caribbean communities and the poor post-school prospects of such students' causing 'behaviour... antagonistic to white teachers' and creating 'perceived counter hostility of white teachers who have to deal with such behaviour and the threat to school order which it poses' (Foster, 1990).

Several researchers have concluded that pupils of Caribbean heritage display more behaviour problems, or are perceived by their teachers to do so (Smith and Tomlinson, 1989. Tizard et al, 1988. Wright, 1985. Mac an Ghail, 1988. Foster, 1990. Brook, 1991). Do teachers' negative and racist attitudes cause poor behaviour and contribute to the different treatment that pupils of Caribbean heritage appear to receive, or is Foster's argument valid?

In Gillborn's study, as discussed on page 132, pupils of Caribbean heritage were unduly disciplined, even those who chose to 'accommodate rather than to challenge teachers' (Gillborn, 1990). The severity of punishments meted out to pupils of Caribbean heritage, whatever their response to teachers, and the vagueness of the reasons for disciplinary action recorded by teachers, also suggest that negative perceptions by teachers must be taken into account and cannot be ruled out as an influence on pupil behaviour.

In another article (1990b), Foster expanded his argument further, arguing that teacher attitudes, if based on preconceived racist stereotyping, would not prevail if they were presented with evidence to the contrary. Moreover, perceptions of a group would not necessarily be translated into unequal treatment directed at an individual nor, he argued, did the evidence available justify a causal link from negative teacher attitudes to unequal treatment. Finally, Foster said, even if teachers do have negative attitudes, these may not be reflected in the classroom.

Foster's argument can be challenged at several levels. The evidence of the studies described in this chapter is consistent with several earlier studies which also suggest that teachers hold stereotypical views of pupils of Caribbean heritage. (See Cohen, 1986 for some of these.) Teachers who subscribe to racist stereotypes may be as inflexible in the presence of evidence contradicting them as are other sectors of the population who accept and are influenced by racist stereotypes (Husband, 1986).

The nature of racism suggests that stereotypical views will not easily change. Stereotyping is not an isolated act of thinking but an integral part of a racist framework which permeates thinking, perceiving, feeling, judging, evaluating, rationalising, acting and interrelating (Figeroa, 1991).

It seems likely, therefore, that teachers who hold negative racist attitudes will be influenced by them in their practice in the classroom and their interaction with pupils and parents. Their prejudices may become self-fulfilling prophecies, especially for young pupils who cannot handle unfair treatment and older students who challenge them. This is not to deny the role of pupils. Very poor behaviour cannot be condoned, even when it is in response to teacher racism.

Assuming that racism cannot be ruled out as a reality, how important is it in children's education? Two of the ten studies described earlier in this chapter suggest that its impact has been exaggerated i.e. Study A by Smith and Tomlinson, and Study G by Foster.

Both studies suffer from inadequate analysis of the ethnic minority experience of racism. As we noted in the last section, people of Caribbean heritage may not readily talk about their experiences and this needs to be taken into account in planning research. In Study A, interviews were not designed to encourage ethnic minority pupils or parents to reveal their experiences. In Foster's study, he appeared to relate more to (white) teachers than to (black) pupils and was unwilling to accept pupils' experiences of racism when they did mention them.

Both studies are open to other criticism. Smith and Tomlinson could not interview teachers, partly because of the sensitivity of the area of research, which made the teachers reluctant to cooperate. And this research, extensive and large scale as it was, made no attempt to incorporate a qualitative analysis to examine racism and its effects on black pupils' experiences.

Foster's study, however, incorporated both teacher interviews and observation. It was unusually thorough in its attempt to cover, comprehensively, all possible aspects of racism and also, unusually, it included a systematic and statistical examination of teacher-pupil interaction between teachers of different curriculum areas and the pupils in one class.

In spite of these strengths, the research design and analysis appeared to have crucial gaps. Ethnic minority community members were not interviewed nor their views sought about racism, even though some were visiting the school to pilot a black studies input to the curriculum.

Ten of the forty teachers were not interviewed and no explanation was offered. Were these teachers 'reluctant to cooperate' with the study? Moreover, teacher interviews included six teachers with some tendency to stereotype pupils, a fact which Foster appeared to discount on the grounds that they were not keen to talk about it.

Some pupils of Caribbean heritage appeared to behave unduly poorly but no attempt was made to examine whether 'race' and background experiences contributed in any way. Foster appeared convinced that poor behaviour was due to the evident student alienation from school. The gap is all the more surprising because of Foster's perception of its implications. According to Foster, the poor behaviour of boys of Caribbean heritage was responsible for their disproportionate number in lower sets and their under-representation in the top sets (Foster, 1990).

It is not clear whether these deficiencies in the research arose from a pre-supposition that alienation is the cause of poor behaviour, from an identification with teachers in a school striving to achieve equal opportunities, from a misunderstanding about the nature of racism and its consequences for pupils of Caribbean heritage, or from a combination of such factors. Whatever the reason, Foster's evidence is insufficient for him to conclude (and without any reservations) that the school was non-racist one.

What conclusions can we draw from this set of studies? It is important to stress that any conclusions can only be tentative. Excluding the work by Smith and Tomlinson and by Tizard et al, the research described together covers only twelve schools and two sixth form colleges. In England there are about 27,000 schools so we cannot generalise from the studies to the country as a whole, and it is impossible to predict the prevalence of non-racist or racist schools in Britain.

However, in the ten studies, the consistency of evidence indicates that teacher racism is a reality in some schools. This conclusion remains valid and is not undermined by the arguments by Foster or Smith and Tomlinson. As for schools where teachers are completely non-racist, I believe that there are some. But, only Foster's study claims to have found such a school and his evidence is not sufficient to justify his claim.

Racism and Achievement

Drawing from the body of research as a whole, the model underlying the work by Wright, Mirza, Mac an Ghail and Gillborn provide the best analysis of the processes operating in secondary schools.

As illustrated below, negative teacher attitudes cause unfavourable treatment of pupils of Caribbean heritage in teacher-pupil relationships:

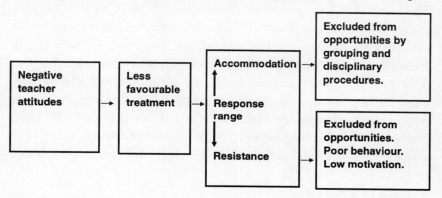

Responses of pupils vary, ranging from resistance and challenging teachers to accommodation, with girls more likely to take the latter line. Whatever the responses, opportunities are restricted through pupil groupings, disciplinary procedures and poor advice. Where pupils do challenge teachers, anti-school behaviour complicates the picture. Opportunities may be reduced further and underachievement become still greater.

For primary age pupils, it is difficult to draw conclusions at this stage because only one relatively recent study analysed teacher attitudes for this age group, and the consequences for pupil responses and pupil achievement were not examined as part of the research (Wright, 1992). In the absence of research, two earlier models are presented below. Both emphasise self-concept, though one also includes expectation:

1. Green (1985)

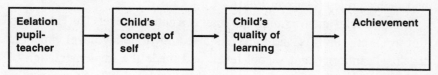

169

2. Syer (1982)

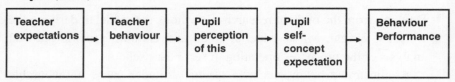

The case studies of young pupils described in this book suggest that these earlier models are simplistic and misleading. Young children's responses to racism are likely to be very diverse, just as they as for older pupils. Experiences may contribute to a lack of confidence for some, but it is unlikely that 'low self-esteem' will be the norm. Nor will it be the only effect. Young children are dependent on the adult in charge of them for reassurance and guidance and, where this is not provided, children's personal and social development may be affected. Racism in schools can affect children's behaviour and motivation and must also be considered.

Racism in Education

This section gives a brief account of trends one needs to consider to decide whether the experience of racism in schools by pupils of Caribbean heritage will alter in the future. Changes in policy need to be examined and also shifts in the nature and concept of 'racism'.

Education policies relevant to 'race' issues have been established centrally and at local government level. During the nineteen eighties, local education authorities increasingly introduced policies for multicultural or anti-racist education and for equal opportunities. These were aimed at improving education generally for all children but were expected to benefit ethnic minority educational experiences and outcomes. While there were relatively few such policies in the mid-nineteen eighties, they had become widespread by the early nineties. Eighty-two out of ninety-one respondents to a questionnaire circulated to 127 authorities in 1993 had such a policy (German,1994).

It is also relevant to examine policies at a national level. The Education Reform Act (1988) is said to have slowed down policy development at the local authority and school level, and made the implementation of multicultural/anti-racist practices variable (Taylor, 1992). Subsequently, in 1992, the Education (Schools) Act formalised the inspection of all schools and included equal opportunities explicitly as part of its framework. While this will undoubtedly have led to some improvement, the effect of the Act was not as beneficial as might have been hoped. The treatment of equal opportunities in the first fifty inspection reports was found to be 'at best unsatisfactory and at worst ignorant' (Runnymede Trust, 1995). Since then the specific focus on equal opportunities has been removed, equal opportunities included at appropriate stages in new guidance materials, and such reference are to be strengthened in a new Framwork following consultation (Department for Education, 1995).

Thus the likelihood of a continuing revival in school policy initiatives because of the prospect of inspection is difficult to predict at the time of writing. Whatever the trend towards initiating policies, these may not have resulted in as great a change in pupils' classroom experiences. There are several reasons for this. For a start, improvements depend on changing teacher attitudes. This takes time and is difficult to achieve. Racism is and has been deeply entrenched and educational policies are often less beneficial than expected (Troyna and Carrington, 1990). A racist frame of reference is deeply ingrained in ways of thinking, feeling, judging, evaluating, rationalising, and of inter-relating, and so is a wide-ranging, powerful and pervasive influence on white teachers (Figueroa, 1991).

Secondly, it is becoming clear that racism is more complex and full of ambiguities than has been realised, affecting groups differently and with gender and class issues interweaving with 'race' issues (Rattansi, 1993). This adds to the difficulties of implementing policies effectively. Thirdly, the commitment of schools to equal opportunities may have lapsed in the nineties because of the pressures and problems of implementing the National Curriculum.

Nevertheless, the increase in local education policies since the eighties is so large that, if even a fraction of these are effective, they must have had a significant impact on school policy initiatives and ethnic minority classroom experiences. On balance therefore, one might expect some improvements compared with the previous decade, though it is likely that only a few schools will have developed to the stage where racist practices have been completely eradicated.

The social context also needs to be considered. The 1993 PSI Survey on education and employment suggested that while some groups have made progress, most noticeably those of Indian, African Asian and

Chinese backgrounds, circumstances for others are little improved (Jones, 1993). Opportunities for gaining professional qualifications and for success thereafter are reduced (Commission for Racial Equality, 1988). Even New Towns are not exempt from racism (Wrench et al, 1993). Incidents of overt harassment against people and property is on the increase.

That racism is still a reality for many is hardly surprising. Belief in the superiority of white British norms had its foundation in the power relationships of the Empire and took hold of the national consciousness (Husband). Stereotypes constructed by this relationship were extrapolated to beliefs in differences in intellectual and moral qualities. While stereotypes might be subject to change over time, their capacity for perpetuating negative attitudes to ethnic minorities have been unchanging and powerful and personal stereotyped views remain inflexible even in the presence of contrary evidence (Husband,1986). So racist views are potentially very pervasive and strong, and much will still have to be done to ensure that racism is reduced.

Changes in the social context may influence racist behaviour and these also need to be considered. The remainder of this section examines changes in the perception of and approaches to racism.

A book entitled *The New Racism* precipitated increasing debate about whether a different form of racism is emerging (Barker, 1981). It has been argued that fewer overtly racist statements are made today and that although more explicit forms of harassment such as those executed by the Far Right do still occur, they are likely to be criticised and seen as unacceptable by a majority of the population. This creates the impression that racism is in decline apart from that manifested by a very small and atypical sector.

In reality, however, racism has become more covert and subtle and is more widespread than it appears to be (Troyna and Carrington, 1990). In the New Racism, the focus is on culture, with negative feelings about minority groups persisting but presented as common-sense fears about 'other' groups or 'outsiders'. The underlying hostility to minority groups is, therefore, justified as fundamental in human nature (Husband, 1986). Consequently the effects of racism — denying, disparaging, dismissing, and excluding people of minority backgrounds — continue as before.

One of the key issues in the new approach has been the concept of 'Britishness'. The exclusion of black British people and their cultures from this notion has been promoted and perpetuated by politicians and others in influential positions such as Kenneth Baker, Norman Tebbit, Keith Joseph and John Major (Troyna and Hatcher, 1991. Gillborn, 1993). In a speech in July 1995, the head of the Schools Curriculum and Assessment Authority, Nick Tate, urged headteachers to instil into pupils 'British culture' — a British culture of a narrow and exclusionist kind, of which Christianity is an essential component. Increasingly, discourse has been deracialised, with ethnic minority communities constructed 'as outsiders ('non-believers') who present a direct challenge to 'our' traditions and faith. The notion of a shared British *culture* (religion and tradition) acts as a proxy for the idea of separate 'races' (Gilborn, 1993).

This allows racist ways of thinking and behaving to be promoted as normal and acceptable. The changing manifestations of racism have created difficulties which, unfortunately, have been compounded by new areas of concern. One example is the debate about European dimensions of racism in which the key issues are identified as the disadvantages and hostility directed towards non-residents of a country i.e. migrant workers and refugees. Another is the increasing interest in 'racisms' and the widening of discussion from 'black' ethnic minorities to all potentially disadvantaged ethnic groups including, for example, the Irish. While important issues, the danger of these developments is that the very real and long-standing problems faced by British people of Caribbean or Asian background might be neglected.

What, then, is the outlook for improved schooling for pupils of Caribbean heritage in this decade, when racism against people of Caribbean heritage in the wider society is continuing and while the manifestation of racism is changing and new focuses take attention away from them?

In the absence of research at this stage, one can only hypothesise. One reaction against the violence of the Far Right might be a greater impetus towards school policies and practices to reduce harassment. This must be to the advantage of pupils of Caribbean heritage. On the other hand, efforts to reflect on and change teacher attitudes may appear less important in the context of the new approach to racism, with its common-sense approach justifying racist attitudes and its fostering of an exclusionist notion of 'Britishness'.

In sum, there have been forces acting to reduce racism in schools, the most important being the increase in the nineteen eighties of local education authority policies. Nevertheless, the outlook is not good. School policies may be ineffective or allowed to die away and there are many reasons — political, philosophical, empirical — which suggest that racism in schools may continue to be a reality in the forthcoming years, with consequences for continuing underachievement among pupils of Caribbean heritage. Unfortunately, and in the absence of research, we have no idea of its scale.

Racist Teachers and Pupil Achievement — Conclusions

This chapter has examined ten studies, carried out in the eighties and early nineties, which throw some light on the nature of racism in schools and its effect on pupils of Caribbean heritage.

The conclusions drawn were that some pupils of Caribbean heritage suffer from educational disadvantages, as compared with other pupils, which are especially evident in inequitable treatment by teachers. The pupils' educational opportunities are reduced as a result, but to differing degrees, depending on the situation and the pupils' responses. Such effects may be compounded by other inequalities, such as unbalanced advice from teachers with stereotypical views, and proportionately greater allocation of pupils of Caribbean heritage to lower ability or less desirable subject groups.

The outlook for the nineteen nineties for pupils of Caribbean heritage continues to warrant concern. The difficulties and the potential tardiness of implementing change in this area have to be viewed in the context of a 'New Racism', more covert but equally harmful, and of a trend for equal opportunities to be targeted towards other groups at the expense of those of Caribbean heritage.

Also justified is the need for more research. The research already published is problematic. There is a paucity of studies and, with no large scale study which effectively examines racism, we have no way of telling how extensive racism is in schools or even what proportion of schools or teachers might be described as 'racist'. Equally, we have no idea how many teachers might justifiably be described as 'positive', i.e. aware of racism and its effects and keen to meet ethnic minority needs.

Furthermore, the research methodology used to date is deficient in many ways. While the conclusion that some pupils of Caribbean heritage are disadvantaged at school is validated by the body of research as a whole, individual pieces of research are open to criticism. It is essential that criteria be developed for reliable qualitative research in this field.

Many of the problems of the research arise from the nature of racism. Those involved have not paid sufficient attention to the complexities of racism and of 'racist encounters', nor allowed adequately for differences in perspective. Once differences in perspective are recognised, the processes used by recipients to interpret encounters and the methods by which racism is enacted in schools must be clearly specified. Researchers will need to consider these processes at all stages of their work i.e. in its design, implementation, analysis and description, and evaluation.

Finally, looking at the model of underachievement and the variables which might be relevant, it is clear that behaviour and pupil motivation are the key pupil variables to consider at the secondary level. Confidence appears to be less important at this stage, because many pupils develop their own goals and criteria for success based on peer group evaluation. Given the treatment meted out to and the vulnerability of younger pupils, confidence is more likely to be a factor for pupils in primary schools, and behaviour appears also to be an important constraint on children's achievement.

Chapter 9

Moving Towards Achievement

Conclusions

Although pupils of Caribbean heritage form a relatively small proportion of the school population in Britain, there are large numbers in schools, about 130,000 aged five to fifteen according to the 1991 census. There is considerable diversity in culture and backgrounds among them in spite of their shared Caribbean ancestry.

These pupils are British, in many cases second generation, yet as a group, they continue to underachieve compared with white British pupils. Chapter 1 reviewed evidence from their lesser achievement, outlining the research studies, analyses of individual education authority's GCSE examinations results, and analyses at a national level of results from the assessments of seven year olds in the National Curriculum.

Research on 'underachievement' dates back to the early sixties but no comprehensive clear answers about its causes or solutions have emerged. Diversions and distractions from specific research on achievement have been partly responsible for this relatively slow progress, and what one researcher has called the 'subsuming' of research on ethnic minorities into other areas may also have played a part (Gillborn, 1993).

A key reason for the lack of meaningful answers after years of research is that this is an area in which it is not easy to be objective. Personal

177

perspectives and experiences may influence the choice of what is researched, the design of the studies, and the resulting analysis and conclusions.

In the past, the focus has been on problems perceived in one 'macro' variable, such as explanations of 'underachievement' that pathologise the child or blame the home or castigate schools for being racist. This has discouraged the growth of a realistic theory in which factors influencing achievement can be positive as well as negative and which incorporates home, pupil and school variables.

The previously unpublished research described in chapters 3 to 7 illustrates that some teachers try to be non-racist and introduce measures to foster academic success. Many parents of Caribbean heritage are supportive and work with teachers towards academic progress. Some pupils of Caribbean heritage are academically successful. A balanced theory must allow for all of this. These chapters, analysing pupil achievement in the 'positive' classrooms in the study, identify home, pupil *and* classroom variables which influence achievement, generally reducing but sometimes promoting it.

The consequences of racism are especially interesting. Children's very real encounters with racism may impinge on their experiences in 'positive' classrooms, affecting their behaviour or confidence and hence their achievement. This compounds the disadvantages young children face when classroom and home cultures differ and cause confusion and behavioural problems or reduce their motivation and interest.

In schools that have racist teachers, pupils of Caribbean heritage may be seriously disadvantaged. The processes involved are complex, as discussed in chapter 8. 'Racist' interpersonal interactions can take a variety of forms. The mechanisms of interpretation used by pupils who are experiencing interpersonal racism are varied. There are myriad factors contributing to potentially lower achievement, especially in the complicated structure of secondary schools. The end result can be that pupils are excluded from the classroom when they do not deserve to be, that they develop behavioural problems and lose confidence and, in many cases, loose their motivation.

A Model of Achievement

This section draws from the research in 'positive' classrooms and the evaluation of research literature on racism, in an attempt to hypothesise a more balanced theory of achievement. As will be seen, the variables included are such that the theory appears relevant to all children regardless of background.

The model suggested focuses on the individual pupil and has as its starting point the tasks done daily by the pupil. The approach is at a micro level and is very different from those based on deficit theories, as represented in the diagram on page 40 and described in chapter 2. Instead of identifying *only* pupils *or* homes *or* schools as the cause of 'under-achievement', all three are deemed relevant. The most immediate role is played by variables which are largely but not exclusively pupil-related.

According to this model, pupil variables determine the day-to-day success in the tasks done in the classroom. The pupil's attainment to date, their motivation, concentration while working, the proportion of time spent not working because they are distracted from the task, and the pupil's ability are all crucial factors. Outcomes depend also on the opportunities provided by the teacher and might be less good if the academic opportunities for learning are poorer than those in tasks given to pupils from other backgrounds. The pupil's level of achievement may be restricted relative to others in the class or, because of inequitable allocation to ability or subject groupings, to others in the same year group.

There are also variables related to the 'whole child' which influence the child's success in classroom tasks and need to be taken into account in the model. Confidence is important since it can help to promote achievement. Personal and social skills and attributes are other determinants. For example, established patterns of taking responsibility, working independently, and relating well to others may promote success, whereas poorly developed skills of this nature may hamper achievement. Children's abilities and strategies for handling different or difficult situations are also contributory factors. Poor behaviour towards others or exhibited for emotional reasons can reduce time on task and inhibit achievement.

Motivation and time on task can also be affected by the pupil's attitude to work. The child's perspective on priorities and how these rate in relation to academic work, need to be considered. It is important therefore to include the pupil's 'agendas' in the model. Lastly, tasks cannot be done if a pupil is not in the classroom. Absence due to frequent lateness and non-attendance are relevant pupil variables. Being out of the classroom due to exclusion by the teacher, for whatever reason and whether justified or not, are also potential barriers to academic success.

The effect of the home also needs to be considered. It has not been possible to examine variables related to the home in any depth in this book, but my case studies indicate certain factors so I have included them in the model, albeit tentatively. The nurture of the child — whether basic needs are met, the amount of love, security and support provided — can all influence the way the child develops. Also hypothesised as playing a part are the guidance on behaviour and taking responsibility, and whether there are clear and consistent boundaries.

Children's personal and social development can be influenced by the examples set by the family in valuing oneself and skills for handling conflict and criticism. The family might contribute to learning by encouraging wide interests and fostering problem-solving cognitive skills involving questioning, reasoning, analysing and finding information. These are all hypothesised as relevant home variables. Whether the family places a high value on education may be relevant, and whether the parents are able and concerned to work in partnership with the school in supporting academic progress.

The model is shown opposite. Task variables, largely pupil-related, are shown in Box 1, home variables in Box 2. It might be argued that the pupil and home variables described are relevant to the achievement of any child regardless of background. This could be said also of the classroom variables, shown in Box 3.

Chapter 6 highlighted the importance of teachers' high expectations of pupils and the need to establish clear standards of work and behaviour. The academic environment is an important influence on the way pupils approach tasks, their motivation and success. Is the environment inspiring and stimulating? Are clear objectives set and individual needs catered for? And, finally, are relevant cultures reflected in the classroom?

The model incorporates other aspects of the classroom environment. Relationships between children, and between teachers and children are very important. Is each child valued, respected, accepted and empathised with by the teacher and do pupils listen to and value each other? Finally,

Box 2 HOME VARIABLES

Provision of basic needs

Love, security, support

Clear boundaries — behaviour, responsibility

Examples — valuing self, handling conflicts

Fostering — interests, cognitive skills

Value, support — education

Box 3 CLASS VARIABLES

Expectations/standard

Academic environment inspiring/stimulating /clear objectives/ individual need

Reflecting culture

Valuing/respect/ acceptance/empathy

Value parental involvement

E

Box 1 THE WHOLE CHILD

Confidence

Personal/social skills

Behaviour

Pupil's agendas

Presence in the classroom

The Task

Attainment to date

Motivation

Concentration on-task

Time on task

Ability

Opportunities provided

PUPIL ACHIEVEMENT

the value of parental involvement was accepted in the five classrooms researched, so this too is part of the model.

A Different Experience

Life in the classroom might be experienced differently by pupils of Caribbean heritage and white pupils and these experiences, sometimes deeply felt, can affect academic progress. This section hypothesises about such lived-through encounters, drawing largely from the research in chapters 3 to 7 and from previous research on racism. That such experiences might be crucial and might lie at the heart of lesser achievement is shown in the model on the previous page where they are indicated in the small circle, E. A magnified version of the circle and of the 'E' factors are shown opposite.

Children's various encounters with racism as experienced in interpersonal relations at school are considered first. The most extreme are those that occur in schools where there are racist teachers. Although nowadays overtly abusive comments are unlikely, racist views still exist and, where this is so, children of Caribbean heritage might be perceived as 'outsiders' and inferior. These children will experience racism at an individual level, even if they are not verbally abused or teased by adults, and they will suffer as a result of cultural racism exhibited by teachers.

Children who have 'positive' teachers in schools at the other end of the awareness continuum are, however, not immune from negative influences at school. Some may have suffered previously from teacher hostility or stereotyping, or be subject currently to negative interactions because of a single racist teacher on the staff of a generally positive school. Other pupils might harass them, traumatising the most vulnerable and affecting others.

There are also encounters in the classroom to consider. With 'positive' teachers, expectations of all pupils may be equally high. Pupils of Caribbean heritage might be generally valued and respected and some provision made for reflecting the children's homes in school. Nevertheless there could be situations which, subtly, give children of Caribbean heritage the feeling that there is something wrong and different about their backgrounds. In times of stress, teachers might show less sympathy for black pupils or their families than they do for white children. These encounters impinge on other children of Caribbean heritage in the class. Some may

ENCOUNTERS

Interpersonal Racism at school
Racism outside school
Racism at second/third hand
Limited resources, pressures on family

OTHER NEGATIVE INFLUENCES

Cultural norms, values — different in school
Everday life practices — not reflected in school
Absence of positive role models
History of poor academic success

COUNTERACTING/POSITIVE INFLUENCES

Valuing of roots
Curriculum — Antiracist/multicultural

identify with the black children and parents concerned, or with the home practices which appear to be the source of teacher irritation. Thus can a perception of difference develop, reinforcing the lack of confidence of sensitive children and arousing anger, frustration, or protectiveness in others.

One can also imagine encounters outside school that can have racist connotations and be hurtful or difficult to handle. Children might be the target of direct racism or experience overt and unpleasant incidents at second hand when incidents involve family members and friends, or at third hand in stories of racist violence elsewhere in Britain. Members of the family might describe indirect racism, discrimination in employment or housing, sometimes with the alleged discrimination corroborated by evidence. Some children may be particularly sensitive to various other messages in society that convey the message that some groups are perceived as inferior.

A few children may suffer indirectly because of pressures at home, as family members suffer from overt racism or struggle to progress despite great hardship. This could impinge on children's well-being in the classroom and make them angry about racism, which could in turn affect their behaviour and motivation.

Cultural differences may have an impact on the learning of young children of Caribbean heritage. There are many sub-cultures to consider. Some of them have values and norms that guide relationships and behaviour which differ from the culture associated with white families. Teachers might not be aware of this and classrooms can portray a culture unfamiliar to some children of Caribbean heritage. Young pupils might find such differences between home and school norms confusing, and their not knowing what is required could lead to poor behaviour and low achievement.

Everyday practices at home might well differ from those familiar to white teachers. Yet, the food, the utensils and decorations used, and other aspects of the home are familiar to every young child and need to be reflected at school. And for children of all ages, their everyday lifestyles and concerns are important and relevant. Schools need to bring these into their teaching.

Schools with a good antiracist/multicultural curriculum for all children will have taken this into account. But progress is slow. Many persist with a monocultural/eurocentric curriculum, failing to offer one to which pupils of Caribbean heritage can relate, thus inadvertently promoting feelings of being different and excluded. Accordingly, some children might lose interest and motivation and the progress of younger pupils could even, in some instances, be slowed by caution and unwillingness to venture into unfamiliar areas.

Teachers are increasingly recognising the importance of role models with whom boys and girls can identify. They see this as motivating, especially for older pupils. One consequence of racism is the dearth of black people in prestigious and higher earning occupations. White teachers might not know about successful black people so they will not appear in images in classrooms. Where all the images are white, the experience of pupils of Caribbean heritage in the classroom will be different from that of white pupils. The effect will be especially serious where there are no black teachers to serve as living role models — as is so often the case. Its effects will be exacerbated in schools with a history of poor success and hence an absence of achieving black pupils and a fostering of feelings of despair or disenchantment.

The case studies in chapter 7 suggest that children of Caribbean heritage can also benefit positively from their Caribbean-ness and these effects should also be considered. A family's valuing of roots can foster children's confidence in their identity, and hence enhance their classroom experiences indirectly. The classroom itself can generate positive influences as, for example, when the curriculum values their backgrounds or encourages children to articulate and handle racist encounters.

Explaining 'Underachievement' and Achievement

Pupils of Caribbean heritage, as a group, appear to 'underachieve'. The model on page 181 is used to examine contributory factors and the connection between 'underachievement' and the 'different experience' discussed above.

The consequences for outcomes may be most severe in schools where individual teachers are racist and negative influences pertaining to variables in Box 3 are likely. Children of Caribbean background can be disadvantaged also in 'positive' schools, nearer to the other end of the teacher awareness spectrum, although the potentially negative influences pertaining to variables in Box 3 are unlikely. Negative influences are still possible and take the form of those represented within the E (page 183), leading to differences in classroom experience and impinging on important variables in Box 1. Confidence may be reduced, personal and social development hindered, and behaviour or motivation suffer.

Achievement of older pupils might be negatively affected because of their experiences when they were younger. Patterns established for variables in Box 1 in previous schooling can persist, contributing to continuing and increasing 'underachievement'. Habits of non-attendance and lateness can become ingrained. Alternative agendas can become more important and behaviour increasingly worse. As pupils get older, the quantity and quality of their work might deteriorate further in comparison with peers and the disparity in attainment increase as students of Caribbean heritage spin down a spiral of academic non-achievement.

In schools where many teachers are racist, the disadvantages for pupils of Caribbean heritage will be even greater. The teachers will probably hold lower academic expectations of pupils of Caribbean heritage, lack tolerance and empathy towards them, expect more behavioural problems, and treat them disrespectfully and with hostility. Rather than showing understanding and equal consideration, they could make wrong and stereotypical assumptions about individual pupils and about cultural differences. These views may be rationalised as 'common sense' and the lesser value placed on these pupils can come to be seen as normal and acceptable. In effect, classroom experiences for these pupils are likely to be predominantly negative and arise directly from the influence of variables shown in Box 3.

The consequences for pupils attending a racist school will differ, depending on the personality and ability of the pupil, on her/his experiences of racism and how they affect the pupil, and on the variables listed in Box 1. Some pupils respond to a racist school environment by rebelling and challenging teachers. Their learning opportunities are minimal, because of unfair grouping arrangements and the shorter time spent in the classroom due to disproportionate exclusions by teachers and their own poor attendance and punctuality. A lethal combination occurs when pupils' agendas exclude academic achievement and teacher-pupil interactions are hostile. The pupils' behaviour and motivation and their time on task inevitably suffer.

The influence of teachers on the academic development of very young pupils is potentially great. Some children may be especially vulnerable and at risk when exposed to racist teachers who, although responsible for their welfare, are hostile to them, pay insufficient attention to settling them down and encouraging them, and prevent them from participating equally in classroom life. The child's behaviour may deteriorate and there can be serious and harmful effects on their confidence and security.

There are also likely to be pupils across the age range who are motivated, sometimes confident, and keen to achieve and to 'avoid problems'. In a racist school they, like other pupils of Caribbean heritage, are likely to suffer unduly and undeservedly from exclusions, allocation to low status groups and to other obstacles to full participation in classroom life. In effect, pupils in racist schools respond very differently to the hostility they face but, whatever their response, they are disadvantaged by reduced opportunities and outcomes.

Most schools are at neither extreme and lie somewhere on the continuum between racist schools and 'positive' schools. In such schools, it is possible that one or more of the teacher variables listed in Box 3 will contribute to negative experiences. The consequences for pupils of Caribbean heritage will be less serious than in racist schools but worse than in 'positive' schools.

Further along the awareness continuum beyond 'positive' schools, there might be no negative encounters in interpersonal relations with teachers or pupils. The curriculum is permeated with a high-profile antiracist ethos and, as a result, pupils learn how to handle and counteract the negative racist encounters experienced outside school. There is trust between parents and teachers, and a willingness to talk openly about children's 'race' and background experiences. In these 'ideal' schools, the chance that pupils of Caribbean heritage, as a group, will underachieve is likely to be minimal.

When considering the causes of 'underachievement', it is important to look also at achievement, sometimes high achievement, and the conditions that nourish it. Clearly the 'ideal' schools will do so, and 'positive' schools can also promote success, as discussed in chapter 4. Occasionally, some pupils may be high achievers even in racist schools where, although potential disadvantage is great and the chance of high achievement low, some 'accommodating' students may succeed despite the odds against them.

Summing up, the model hypothesised tries to encompass the range of factors explaining why pupils of Caribbean heritage perform less well than other groups. Some reasons are related to teachers and to the negative influences from variables listed in Box 3 and these have especially serious consequences when racist teachers regard children of Caribbean heritage and their families as 'outsiders', are hostile, and hold stereotypical views. Others factors arise from the 'different' experiences of pupils of Caribbean heritage, which can occur even when teachers are less racist. Such experiences may influence variables listed in Box 1 and reduce performance in classroom tasks. There are also pupils in similar circumstances who achieve to the full and the model attempts to account for this possibility.

187

'School Effects'

The school attended by a pupil is highly likely to influence the educational outcomes for the pupil. Several aspects of schools need to be considered in an examination of such 'school effects' for pupils of Caribbean heritage. This book has been designed to focus on those relating to 'race' and background issues, examining the experiences of pupils of Caribbean heritage in classrooms and what teachers can do to promote their achievement. The study necessarily excludes other potentially important school effects.

One relevant variable to consider is the standard of achievement for all pupils in the school — the 'school effect' emphasised in the third deficit theory. Chapter 2, which examined this theory, suggested that its underlying assumption that 'poor schools are the sole cause of 'underachievement'' is implausible. Whatever the quality of education on offer for all pupils, the achievement of pupils of Caribbean background may suffer because of the 'E' factors. Nevertheless the part played by 'poor' schools in contributing to 'underachievement' needs further examination for, if pupils of Caribbean heritage are concentrated in poor schools, this will exacerbate and add to their difficulties. To assess the overall effect of poor schools, we need data we do not yet have on the proportion of pupils of Caribbean heritage attending such schools, and on the experiences of these pupils.

Another 'school effect' which needs examination in future research is the ethnic composition of the school attended and its consequences for 'E' factors. It is possible that, everything else being the same, the experiences of pupils of Caribbean heritage in schools with large numbers from the same background might be less negative than in schools with relatively few. The field work described in chapters 3 to 7 was done in schools with some small and some large proportions of pupils of Caribbean heritage in a class, in the hope of clarifying some of these issues. But the sample of schools was small and the teachers themselves and also the schools differed, and this made it virtually impossible to isolate the effect caused by the proportion of pupils of Caribbean heritage in the class. So these influences are not considered, as they were not in the scope of this study.

School-Focused Strategies for Increasing Achievement

In the late nineteen eighties, the impetus for strategies to increase equal opportunities came from several sources. While the interest and momentum may have come from some teachers and schools, local education authority policies or initiatives were frequently a key factor and, in some cases, parental or community pressures may well have played a part.

This section outlines the implications this book has for school development planning and gives examples of how local authority staff or consultants might advise and support schools in responding to the findings described here. It concentrates on what schools can do rather than on the potential role of parents.

The section 'Explaining 'Underachievement' and Achievement' indicates clearly that planning for achievement must take into account the location of each school along the continuum from racist to ideal. For schools with several racist teachers, initiatives have to aim to eliminate the negative influences of the variables listed in Box 3. Whereas in 'positive' schools, one could expect to focus directly on increasing pupils' achievement. The discussion starts by considering schools that have a number of racist teachers.

Here, the process of discussion and planning will need to be considered very carefully. It will be evident to an objective consultant that, from certain remarks made about the pupils and their families, negative views and perceptions are held about those of Caribbean heritage. Such comments should be questioned and careful attention paid to the perspective of pupils and parents of Caribbean heritage. Ensuring the participation of the staff and their commitment to the plan is crucial, and the chance of success greater if initial discussions with the staff identified areas of concern to teachers and specified research targets which can increase teacher knowledge and have practical outcomes.

It seems likely that in some schools where there are racist teachers, pupils of Caribbean heritage will be perceived as causing particularly great problems and the teachers will focus on their behaviour. The consultant might suggest that the school development plan include investigating disciplinary incidents occuring over one particular term and have as its objective improved procedures and a reduction in such incidents.

Targets could include documenting incidents with accounts by all the pupils involved, by their parents and by observers. At the beginning of the planning period, staff could identify the questions they thought useful. For instance: How many and which pupils of ..... background are involved in major behaviour incidents in the course of a term? What exactly happens during each incident? Where and when do they occur? In which situations are pupils excluded from the classroom or school? In which situations is the problem resolved? Are there any patterns in the pupils' perceptions of the causes of problems and how they might be resolved?

Since the perspectives and experiences of everyone involved will differ, the experience and skill of the consultant is an essential element for ensuring that the collection and analysis of data is carried out calmly, objectively and with a view to finding solutions. Only then might the strategy succeed.

In some schools, other areas, too, might be tackled, for example, levels of achievement. The teachers might reveal stereotypical perceptions of culture and difference, such as the consequences for single parent families among those of Caribbean heritage. Setting up a pilot project for increasing achievement might be the most suitable objective. The school development plan could perhaps include case studies of a sample of children, some of them from single parent families, and collecting a balanced selection of published research about achievement.

This might help to dispel some incorrect assumptions by answering questions such as: Is it true that children from single parent families are necessarily disadvantaged? What factors contribute to attainment among the sample? What are the views of pupils and parents of Caribbean heritage on achievement? Is it true at the school or generally that most families of Caribbean heritage live with one parent? Cultural issues are very sensitive, and as prone to misinterpretation as issues involving behaviour. Again the role of the consultant would be crucial.

The context and content of planning would be different for schools further along the continuum towards the ideal. Initiatives could draw on the wealth of experience gained in developing equal opportunities policies and action plans by the process of discussion, questioning and review of different aspects of school life. It is usual to include questions about the ethos of the school, aspects of classroom management, and the perspectives reflected in resources and the taught curriculum. Most guidance documents also include questions about equality of academic outcomes, the extent and quality of home/community-school links, racial harassment at school and the ethnic composition of teaching and non-teaching staff and governors.

Such documents can be used to establish the starting point for the school development plan by identifying its current strengths and weaknesses, and deciding 'where the school wants to go' on the basis of current priorities and the interests of the staff.

Some schools might decide to take a very positive approach, building on areas identified as their strengths. For example, a school with initiatives towards a multicultural curriculum might decide to focus on the contributions of those of Caribbean heritage and to ensure that displays do not exclude such a perspective. Schools prioritising home-school links might decide to ensure that parents of Caribbean heritage are well represented and that contacts and knowledge about these families increases. Alternatively, schools might decide to look at more negative problem areas e.g. finding out about harassment outside school and developing policies to handle harassment at school.

What about schools where teachers are 'positive'? These are schools which take an interest in meeting needs, whose learning resources and stories reflect a range of backgrounds, and which initiate multicultural projects in the curriculum. This book suggests that schools of this kind need to continue to develop their ideas on the education of pupils of Caribbean heritage, with a greater emphasis on achievement and teacher strategies for enhancement.

The plan might include targeting staff meetings or inset days to share ideas and discuss how individual teachers promote achievement for all the pupils in their class and what, if anything, they do to promote the achievement of pupils of Caribbean heritage. It should also include increasing parental involvement for identifying and meeting the pastoral needs of young pupils and for counteracting the backlog of potential problems of older pupils. Within this direct focus on achievement, systems and structures should be established for monitoring the achievement of the different ethnic minority groups.

The school might also decide to examine how the pupils' achievement is influenced by the experiences they have because of being black and their Caribbean backgrounds — i.e. arising from racism and the excluding of their culture from school life. Teachers could take on action research with targeted pupils and collect evidence to reflect further on such issues, as was done in chapter 7, providing of course that this is acceptable to parents. Ideally, parents and teachers will talk openly together about children's 'race' and background experiences, and white teachers benefit from the insight of parents on the matter. It is essential that the research is done carefully and sensitively.

Alternatively, teachers might decide that what is required is a sharper focus on curriculum development to incorporate Caribbean roots and black British experiences regularly in ongoing school topics. A bank of resources and better informed teachers would ensure that, despite all the pressures on teachers today, pupils would have greater access to the curriculum through more effective antiracist/multicultural education.

How effective are the strategies suggested likely to be? Given the strength and power of stereotypes and stereotypical thinking, change is very unlikely to occur where staff are almost all racist, especially if this is true of the Head or key management staff. Action by parents, reinforced by support from local community organisations and Race Equality Councils and, ultimately, the Commission for Racial Equality offer the only chance of success. In less intransigent schools, success will depend on discussions being open and non-confrontational but encouraging the challenging of stereotypes. If there are a few staff who are able to recognise the potentially racist scenarios and raise certain practical questions, and a consultant skilled enough to develop good relations with the staff, promote a balanced discussion of issues and handle the possibly emotional responses, the chances will be greater that some racist staff will begin to rethink their ideas.

Whatever the type of school, its success in reducing racism and raising the achievement of pupils of Caribbean heritage will depend on its effectiveness in managing change. Change is never easy but success is more likely if the facilitators and organisers ensure that there are clear achievable targets, that the plan incorporates methods for their achievement, that it specifies the time period for implementation and monitoring, and that specific individuals are made responsible for particular aspects of the plan. It also helps to set up structures to ensure commitment, time and resources. Some schools have depended on a working party, others on a teacher with special responsibility, yet others on a senior member of staff who has the commitment and power in the school to lead change. Finally and importantly in this area where attitudes, beliefs and emotions are involved, it is essential that every adult working in or with the school actively participates.

A Note on Research Methodology

Arguments and misunderstandings about methodology have hindered progress in this area of research in issues of education and 'race'. There is a need for both quantitative and qualitative methods, but research will only be productive if researchers review the merits and potential disadvantages of each method, discuss together when and how each is most appropriate and disseminate their conclusions.

With quantitative methods, the variables thought to account for changes in the variable being investigated, the dependent variable, are represented in an equation such as:

$Y = aX_1 + bX_2 + cX_3 + ...u$ where Y is the dependant variable,
X_1, X_2, X_3, are the explanatory variables,
u is the residual or error term.

The value and status of the method arise from the fact that whether the individual variables $X1, X2, X3...$ are important and whether they together account for a significant amount of the variation in Y, can be tested statistically. There are however, difficulties which are sometimes not fully understood, which warrant discussion here.

It is impossible to prove causality. Statistical techniques can show that changes in Y, in this case achievement, are associated with changes in X variables identified, but they cannot prove that changes in X *result* in changes in Y. A second point to bear in mind arises from the new model presented in this book. Many of the explanatory X variables are qualitative, their interaction complex, and their relevance dependent on the specific pupil concerned. Researchers need to think about whether, in view of this, a simplistic mathematical model is appropriate and whether the statistical tests based on this approach are valid.

There are also implications for the sort of analysis which can be done. As discussed in previous chapters, researchers have attempted to separate the effects of 'race' and background from those of gender and social class using covariance analysis. In the new model presented in this book, all of these influence children's experiences and, through the 'E' factors, all influence variables listed in Box 1. When this is the case, it may not be possible to isolate the effects of 'race' and background effects from those of gender and class. Researchers need to discuss this issue further.

When presenting and publicising their work, researchers should also be clear about their research objectives and the data analysed. Quantitative methodology is increasingly employed in comparing the effectiveness of schools and the use of league tables. Where this is done, the analysis usually focuses on the progress of pupils, but results showing ethnic differences in progress are presented as, or often mistaken for, conclusions about differences in levels of achievement.

Qualitative methodology has been misrepresented and undervalued in comparison with quantitative techniques. Yet it has the advantage of helping to identify relevant explanatory variables, the processes at work and to construct a model of them. The method uses logical inference to clarify and justify conclusions and this is as acceptable as the statistical methods of quantitative methodology (Mitchell, 1983).

My main reservation is that for this approach to be valid, research and researchers have to adhere to guidelines for its use and the evaluation of the studies. As discussed at length in chapter 8, this is a difficult research area and great care needs to be taken in designing studies, analysing the data collected and presenting and justifying conclusions. Having said this, there is a need for more research of this nature in classrooms, in both 'positive' and less aware primary classrooms, and in secondary classrooms in schools which are more aware of and trying to meet the needs of ethnic minority pupils.

Summing Up

Research has provided us with no conclusive answers to date. This has been of concern to many schools and parents, especially as 'underachievement' has persisted. It is particularly crucial in the nineteen nineties, since all children have legal entitlement to the national curriculum and attainment in it is measured and emphasised as a priority. This study has suggested that the deficit approach in previous theoretical models is incorrect, that the research methodology used has sometimes been flawed, and that other research priorities, and differences in perspective have all hindered progress.

If we want to make real progress, we will need to review our quantitative methodology and take more care in presenting conclusions. Qualitative methodology, a relatively new approach in this area of research, has been useful but needs further refinement before we undertake the additional research required.

This book proposes a new model of achievement on the basis of new research in 'positive' classrooms and a review of the literature on racist schools. The new theory is more balanced than those used previously. It incorporates the effects of those teachers who are aware of racism and cultural differences, as well as of teachers who have a racist frame of reference. It takes into account a variety of factors associated with pupils, which can have positive as well as negative effects on pupil achievement. In accordance with results from the new data, neither homes/families nor pupils are seen as negative and problematic.

The model highlights the need in school development planning and practice to take into account the level of ethnic awareness of the teachers concerned. It is a pastoral model, stressing that achievement depends on the appropriate development of the whole child. Central to the model are children's experiences in the classroom, the effect of these experiences on their outcomes, and the uniqueness of each child in the way that this affects their life chances.

References

Ainscough, M. and Muncey, J. (1989) Meeting Individual Needs, London: Fulton

Ashrif, S. (1994) Personal, Cultural and Institutional Racism, Unpublished Paper

Bagley, C. (1972) Deviant Behaviour in English and West Indian Children, Research in Education 8

Bagley, C., Bart, M. and Wong, J. (1978) Cognition and Success in West Indian 10-year olds in London: A Comparative Study, Educational Studies 4.1

Bagley, C., Mallik, K., and Verma G. (1979) Pupil Self-esteem: A Study of Black and White Teenagers in British Schools, in Bagley, C. and Verma, G. K., Race, Education and Identity, London: Macmillan

Bagley, C. A. (1992) A 'Life History' of White Racism, in Leicester, M. and Taylor, M., Ethics, Ethnicity and Education, London: Kogan Page

Barker, M. (1981) The New Racism: Conservatives and the Ideology of the Tribe, London: Junction Books

Berry, J. (1986) The Literature of the Black Experience, in Sutcliffe, D. and Wong, A., The Language of the Black Experience, Cultural Expression through Word and Sound in the Caribbean and Black Britain, Oxford: Basil Blackwell

Black Peoples Progressive Association and Redbridge Community Relations Council (1978) Cause for Concern: West Indian Pupils in Redbridge, Ilford: Black Peoples Progressive Association and Redbridge Community Relations Council

Brighouse, T. and Tomlinson, J. (1991) Successful Schools, Institute for Public Policy Research Education and Training Paper No. 4, London: Institute of Public Policy Research

Brook, K.,A. (1991) The Effect of Race on the Performance of Black Pupils, Observations of a Single Class Taught by Seven Different Teachers, M Ed Dissertation, University of Birmingham, Unpublished

Burgess, R. (1985) Field Methods in the Study of Research, Lewes: The Falmer Press

Bygott, D. (1992) Black and British, Oxford: Oxford University Press

Carter, T. (1986) Shattering Illusions: West Indians in British Politics, London: Lawrence and Wishart

Cassidy, F. G. (1971) Jamaica Talk, Three Hundred Years of the English Language in Jamaica, London: Macmillan

Chevannes, M. and Reeves, F. (1987) The Black Voluntary School Movement: Definition, Context and Prospects, in Troyna, B. (ed) Racial Inequality in Education, London: Tavistock

Clarke, E. (1966) My Mother Who Fathered Me, London: George Allen and Unwin Ltd (Also see chapter in Lowenthal (1971) op. cit.)

Coard, B. (1971) How the West Indian Child is made Educationally Sub-Normal in the British School System, London: New Beacon Books

Cohen, L. and Cohen, A. (1986) Multicultural Education, A Sourcebook for Teachers, London: Harper & Row

Cohen, C. and Manion, L. (1989) Research Methods in Education, London: Routledge

Commission for Racial Equality (1985) Birmingham Local Education Authority and Schools, Referrals and Suspension of Pupils, London: Commission for Racial Equality

Commission for Racial Equality (1988) Medical School Admissions: Report of a Formal Investigation, London: Commission for Racial Equality

Conner, C. (1991) Assessment and Testing in the Primary School, Lewes: Falmer

Connolly, P. (1992) Playing it by the Rules: The Politics of Research, in 'Race' and Education, British Educational Research Journal, 18.2

Consortium for Assessment and Testing in Schools (1991) Evaluation Report, The Pilot Study of Standardised Assessment Tasks for Key Stage 1, A Report by the Consortium for Assessment and Testing in Schools, London: Schools Examination and Assessment Council

Cottle, T. (1978) Black Testimony: The Voices of Britain's West Indians, London: Wildwood House

Dabydeen, D. and Samaroo, B. (1987) India in the Caribbean, London: Hansib Publishing Ltd

Dalphinis, M. (1986) French Creoles in the Caribbean and Britain, in Sutcliffe, D. and Wong, A., The Language of the Black Experience, Cultural Expression through Word and Sound in the Caribbean and Black Britain, Oxford: Basil Blackwell

Dawson, A. (1988) Inner City Adolescents: Unequal Opportunities, in Verma, G. and Pumfrey, P., Educational Attainments, Issues and Outcomes in Multicultural Education, Lewes: Falmer Press

Delamont, S. (1992) Field Work in Educational Settings, Lewes: Falmer Press

Department of Education and Science (1981) West Indian Children in our Schools, Interim Report of the Committee of Enquiry into the Education of Children from Ethnic Minority Groups, London: HMSO (Rampton Report)

Department of Education and Science (1985) Education for All, Final Report of the Committee of Enquiry into the Education of Children of Ethnic Minority Groups, London: HMSO (Swann Report)

Department of Education and Science, Her Majesty's Inspectorate (1992) The Annual Report of HM Senior Chief Inspector of Schools

Department for Education, Office for Standards in Education (1993 a) Education for Disaffected Pupils, London: Department for Education Publications Centre

Department for Education, Office for Standards in Education (1993 b) Handbook for the Inspection of Schools, London: HMSO

Department for Education (1993 c) Access and Achievement in Urban Education, London: HMSO

Department for Education, Office for Standardisation Education (1995) The New Framework, London: Ofsted

Dodgson, E. (1984) Motherland, West Indian Women to Britain in the 1950s, Oxford: Heinemann Educational Books

Drew, D. and Gray, J. (1990) The Fifth Year Examination Achievements of Black Young People in England and Wales, Educational Research 32.3

Drew, D. and Gray, J. (1991) The Black-White Gap in Examination Results; A Statistical Critique of a Decade's Research, New Community 17.2

Driver, G. (1982) Ethnicity and Cultural Competence, Aspects of Interaction in Multiracial Classrooms, in Bagley, C. and Verma, G.K., Self-Concept, Achievement and Multicultural Education, London: Macmillan

Edwards, V. and Furlong, M. (1985) Reflections on the Language of Teaching, in Burgess, R., Field Methods in the Study of Education, Lewes: Falmer Press

Figueroa, P (1991) Education and the Social Construction of 'Race', London: Routledge

Foster, P. (1990 a) Policy and Practice in Multicultural and Anti-Racist Education, London: Routledge

Foster, P. (1990 b) Cases not Proven: An evaluation of Two Studies of Teacher Racism, British Educational Research Journal 16.4

Foster, P. (1991) Teacher Attitudes and Afro/Caribbean Educational Attainment, Unpublished Paper

German, G. (1992) Multicultural/ Antiracist/ Equal Opportunities Policy, Unpublished Paper

Gillborn, D. (1990) 'Race', Ethnicity, Education. Teaching and Learning in Multi-Ethnic Schools, London: Unwin Hyman

Gillborn, D. (1993) Racism and Antiracism in Real Schools, Milton Keynes: Open University Press

Goldman, R. J. and Taylor, F. M. (1966) 'Coloured Immigrant Children: A Survey of Research Studies and Literature on their Educational Problems and Potential In Britain, Educational Research 8.3

Graham, P. J. and Meadows, C. E. (1967) Psychiatric Disorders in the Children of West Indian Immigrants, Journal of Child Psychology and Psychiatry 8

Green, P. A. (1985) Multi-Ethnic Teaching and the Pupils' Self- Concept, in Department of Education and Science, Education for All, Final Report of the Committee of Enquiry into the Education of Children of Ethnic Minority Groups, London: HMSO

Gundara, J. (1982) Approaches to Multicultural Education, in Tierney, op.cit.

Hammersley, M. and Atkinson, P. (1983) Ethnography, Principles in Practice, London: Tavistock Publications

Hendriques, F. M. (1953) Family and Colour in Jamaica, London: Eyre and Spottiswoode

Herrnstein, R. J. and Murray, C. (1994) The Bell Curve, London: Macmillan

Hessari, R. and Hill, D. (1989) Practical Ideas for Multicultural Learning and Teaching in the Primary School, London: Routledge

Hopkins, D. (1985) A Teacher's Guide to Classroom Research, Milton Keynes: Open University Press

Horowitz, M. M. (Editor) (1971) Peoples and Cultures of the Caribbean, New York: The Natural History Press

Husband, C. (1986) Racism, Prejudice and Social Policy, in Coombe, V. and Little, A. (Editors), Race and Social Work, A Guide to Training, London: Tavistock Publications

Hyder, (Nehaul) K. (1985) Education in the Motherland, Dissertation for Further Professional Studies Certificate in Education, University of Bristol/ Westminster College, Unpublished

Hyder, (Nehaul) K. (1993) The Role of Teachers and Schools in Increasing Access to Higher Education, in Goulbourne, H. and Lewis-Meeks, P., Access of Ethnic Minorities to Higher Education in Britain: A Report of a Seminar at King's College, Cambridge, University of Warwick Centre for Research in Ethnic Relations Occasional Paper in Ethnic Relations Number 10, Coventry: University of Warwick Centre for Research In Ethnic Relations

Inner London Education Authority Research and Statistics Branch (1990) Differences in Examination Performance, RS 1277/90, London: ILEA Research and Statistics

Jones, Trevor (1993) Britain's Ethnic Minorities, London: Policy Studies Institute

Lowenthal, D. (1971) Peoples and Cultures of the Caribbean, An Anthropological Reader, New York: The Natural History Press

Lowenthal, D. (1978) West Indian Societies, London: Oxford University Press for Institute of Race Relations

Mac an Ghail, M. (1988) Young, Gifted and Black, Milton Keynes: Open University Press

Mac an Ghail, M. (1992) Coming of Age in 1980s England, Reconceptualizing Black Students' Schooling Experience, in Gill, D., Mayor, B., and Blair, M. (Editors), Racism and Education, Structures and Strategies, London: Sage

Mackintosh. N. J. and Mascie-Taylor, C. G. N. (1985) The IQ Question, in Department of Education and Science (1985), op. cit.

McIntyre, D., Bhatti, G., Fuller, M. (1993) Educational Experiences of Ethnic Minority Students in the City of Oxford, Oxford Paper in Education, Oxford: Oxford University Department of Educational Studies

Maxime, J. E. (1986) Some Psychological Models of Black Self- Concept, in Ahmed, S., Cheetham, J. and Small, J., Social Work with Black Children and their Families, London: Batsford

Milner, D. (1975) Children and Race, Harmondsworth: Penguin

Mirza, H. (1992) Young, Female and Black, London: Routledge

Mitchell, J., C. (1983) Case and Situation Analysis, The Sociological Review

Mitchener, J. A. (1989) Caribbean, London: Secker & Warburg

Mortimore, P., Sammons, P., Stoll, L., Lewis, L., and Ecob, R. (1988) School Matters: The Junior Years, Wells: Open Books

National Federation for Educational Research / Bishop Grossetestse College Consortium (1992) National Curriculum Assessment at Key Stage 1, 1992 Evaluation, A Report by the NFER/BGC Consortium, London: SEAC, Unpublished

Owen, D. (1992) Ethnic Minorities in Great Britain: Settlement Patterns, Centre for Research In Ethnic Relations National Ethnic Minority Data Archive 1991 Census Statistical Paper No. 1, Coventry: University of Warwick Centre for Research in Ethnic Relations

Peach, C (1991) The Caribbean in Europe: Contrasting Patterns of Migration and Settlement in Britain, France and the Netherlands, Centre for Research in Ethnic Relations Research Paper in Ethnic Relations No. 15, Coventry: University of Warwick Centre for Research In Ethnic Relations

Rattansi, A. (1992) Changing the Subject? Racism, Culture and Education, in Donald, J. and Rattansi, A., 'Race', Culture and Difference, London: Sage Publications

Rose, E. J. B. in association with Deakin, N., Abrams, M., Jackson, V., Peston, M., Vanags, A. H., Cohen, B., Gaitskell, J., and Ward, P. (1969) Colour and Citizenship, A Report on British Race Relations, London: Oxford University Press

Runnymede Trust (1995) Tales of the Unexpected, London: Runnymede Trust

Rutter, M., Yule, W., Berger, M., Yule, B., Morton, J. and Bagley, C. (1974) Children of West Indian Immigrants -I. Rates of Behavioural Deviance and of Psychiatric Disorder, Journal of Child Psychology and Psychiatry and Allied Disciplines 15

Rutter, M., Yule, W., Berger, M., Yule, B., Morton, J., and Bagley, C., (1975) 'Children of West Indian Immigrants -III. Home Circumstances and Family Patterns', Journal of Child Psychology and Psychiatry 16

Rutter, M., Maughan, B., Mortimore, P. and Ouston, J. (1979) Fifteen Thousand Hours, London: Open Books

Sammons, P. (1995) Gender, Ethnic and Socio-Economic Differences in Attainment and Progress, British Educational Research Journal 21.5

Scarr, S., Caparulo, B. K., Ferman, M., Tower, R. B. and Caplan, J. (1983) Developmental Status and School Achievements of Minority and Non-Minority Children from Birth to 18 Years in a British Midlands Town, British Journal of Developmental Psychology 1

Smith, D. J., and Tomlinson, S. (1989) The School Effect. A Study of Multi-Racial Comprehensives, London: Policy Studies Institute

Stone, M. (1981) The Education of the Black Child in Britain: The Myth of Multicultural Education, London: Collins

Sunday Times (1994) Young Black Pupils Top of the Class in 3 R's, Sunday Times 4.12.94

Syer, M. (1982) Racism, Ways of Thinking and School, in Tierney, op. cit.

Taylor, M. (1981) Caught Between, Slough: National Foundation for Educational Research and Nelson

Taylor, M. (1992) Multicultural Antiracist Education after ERA, Slough: National Federation for Educational Research

Tierney, J. (1982) Race, Migration and Schooling, London: Holt Rinehart and Winston

Tizard, B., Blatchford, P., Burke, J., Farquhar, C., and Plewis, I. (1988) Young Children at School in the Inner City, Hove, Sussex: Lawrence Erlbaum Assocaiates

Tomlinson, S. (1983) Ethnic Minorities in British Schools, London: Heinemann

Tomlinson, S. (1990) Effective Schooling for Ethnic Minorities, New Community 16.3

Troyna, B. (Editor) (1987) Racial Inequality in Education, London: Tavistock Publications

Troyna, B. and Carrington, B. (1990) Education, Racism and Reform, London: Routledge

Troyna, B. and Hatcher, R. (1991) British Schools for British Citizens?, Oxford Review of Education, 17.3

University of Leeds School of Education (1991) Evaluation of National Curriculum Assessment at Key Stage 1 (ENCA), Leeds: School of Education, University of Leeds

Verma, G. K.(1990) Identity, Education and Black Learners: Are Things improving? Multicultural Teaching 8.3

Wrench, J., Brah, H. and Martin, P. (1993) Invisible Minorities, Racism in New Towns and New Contexts, Monographs in Ethnic Relations No. 6, Coventry: University of Warwick Centre For Research In Ethnic Relations

Wright, C. (1985) 1: Learning Environment or Battleground, and II: Who Succeeds at School and Who Decides?, Multicultural Teaching 4.1

Wright, C. (1987) Black Students — White Teachers, in Troyna, B. (Editor), Racial Inequality in Education, London: Tavistock Publications

Wright, C. (1992) Race relations in the Primary School, London: David Fulton

INDEX